Splendid Flowers
for
Every Day

Splendid Flowers
for
Every Day

BY CINDY SMITH

STERLING/CHAPELLE
An imprint of Sterling Publishing Co., Inc.

New York / London
www.sterlingpublishing.com

Chapelle, Ltd.:

If you have any questions or comments, please contact:
  Chapelle, Ltd., Inc., P.O. Box 9252, Ogden, UT 84409
  (801) 621-2777 • (801) 621-2788 Fax
  e-mail: chapelle@chapelleltd.com
  Web site: www.chapelleltd.com

  A Red Lips 4 Courage book
  Red Lips 4 Courage Communications, Inc.:
  8502 E. Chapman Ave., 303
  Orange, CA 92869
  www.redlips4courage.com

Library of Congress Cataloging-in-Publication Data available

Smith, Cindy.
  Splendid flowers for every day / Cindy Smith.
      p. cm.
  "A Sterling/Chapelle book."
  Includes index.
  ISBN 1-4027-2514-0
1. Flower arrangement. I. Title.

  SB449.S546 2005
  745.92--dc22

                                          2005009323

10 9 8 7 6 5 4 3 2 1
Published by Sterling Publishing Co., Inc.
387 Park Ave. South, New York, NY 10016
©2005 By Cindy Smith
Distributed in Canada by Sterling Publishing
c/o Canadian Manda Group, 165 Dufferin St.
Toronto, Ontario, Canada M6K 3H6
Distributed in the United Kingdom by GMC Distribution Services
Castle Place, 166 High Street, Lewes, East Sussex, England BN7 1XU
Distributed in Australia by Capricorn Link (Australia) Pty. Ltd.
P. O. Box 704, Windsor, NSW 2756, Australia
Printed and Bound in China
All Rights Reserved

Sterling   ISBN-13: 978-1-4027-2514-2 Hardcover
             ISBN-10: 1-4027-2514-0

             ISBN-13: 978-1-4027-4961-2 Paperback
             ISBN-10: 1-4027-4961-9

For information about custom editions, special sales, premium and corporate purchases, please contact Sterling Special Sales Department at 800-805-5489 or specialsales@sterlingpub.com

Foreword

For the Love of Flowers

Icome from frugal beginnings and I have the heart and soul of a Midwesterner. Yet I find myself working in an exclusive floral studio serving Hollywood and Beverly Hills—in a world quite different from my own. I design for celebrities.

The rich and famous celebrate birthdays, marriages, and the impending births of their babies just as we do. They simply celebrate life's special moments on a grander scale with a larger price tag and a lot of drama attached. It takes a cast of many to pull off a celebrity celebration and I get to be one of those who help create those temporary flights of fantasy. When cost is of no concern, imaginations are allowed to run wild and nothing is deemed impossible. Flowers flow in abundance.

Because I have been behind the scenes of grand events I have the luxury of knowing how things are done. I have had the pleasure of working with celebrities including Clint Black, Brooke Shields, Jessica Simpson, and Tori Spelling, helping them create memorable occasions.

Throughout this book I share trade secrets that allow you to adapt a few of our designs for the stars for your own celebrations—but with your budgets and readily available materials in mind.

As you begin your journey through the floral abundance of the rich and famous, keep in mind that you too can create the same drama—but without the steep price.

Contents

5 Foreword

8 Introduction

14 Chapter 1

A Birthday Celebration

30 Chapter 2

An Anniversary Celebration

48 Chapter 3

A Reunion Celebration

58 Chapter 4

A Wedding Celebration

84 Chapter 5

A Graduation Celebration

92 Chapter 6

A Friendship Celebration

106 Chapter 7

A Cultural Celebration

116 Chapter 8

A New Life Celebration

137 About the Author

138 Acknowledgments

140 Resources

142 Index

Flowers Through the Ages

There is an Old Dutch proverb that implores us: "If you have but two guilder, spend one on a loaf of bread to feed the body but spend the second on a hyacinth to feed the soul."

It is easy to say, "Flowers are gorgeous." But have you ever seen a flower through the lens of a magnifying glass? Each and every flower is an exquisite work of art. We think that Nature created her extensive collection of flowers expressly for our pleasure. In reality, her prime concern was the proliferation of the species.

The amazing array of colors, shapes, textures, and fragrances found in the flower world are designed specifically to attract bees and butterflies. These little creatures expedite the transfer of pollen that ensures the formation of seeds and the continuation of the flower line. Because of our penchant for flowers, mankind has unknowingly acted as the right hand of Nature, helping her scatter her seeds and plants over the face of the earth.

Many of our ancestors came to America's shores with precious flower seeds from their homeland in their pockets. Thomas Jefferson was so taken with the spectacular sight and aroma of French lilac that he was compelled to bring back cuttings from France for his gardens at Monticello.

Apparently, Napoleon's standing order to his troop captains required them to take back to France any unusual rose species they found growing on foreign soil for his wife's rose garden. Josephine's gardens were held in such high regard in Europe that her head gardener and his plants were allowed to travel unimpeded through enemy lines.

The allure of flowers cuts across cultures and time. We can trace the history of flowers and their significance in people's lives through all of the ages of man—from ancient Egypt to today. We have available to us an impressive collection of artifacts portraying flowers and their uses, and

writings giving credence to what we think we see portrayed. Even the appearance of roses painted on the walls of a pharaoh's tomb is explained in hieroglyphics. It has even been written that Cleopatra wiped out fields of life-sustaining wheat to plant her favorite pink roses so she could perfume her ship's sails with their fragrant oils.

Looking at remnants of times long passed, it becomes obvious that people have always found pleasure in surrounding themselves with flowers either by planting gardens or by cutting blossoms and bringing them inside. Records show that there were 2,000 public gardens in the city of Rome before its fall in 476 A.D. The Hanging Gardens of Babylon, built by Nebuchadnezzar for his queen, were among the Seven Wonders of the Ancient World.

People have always loved a celebration—the more pageantry and symbolism involved the better. Flowers have always played specific roles in the festivities. Celebrations were so frequent and flagrant in the days of the Roman Empire that patricians retained artisan-florists on their staffs to make the necessary garlands and festoons.

Today, celebrations like Valentine's Day and Mother's Day continue to exert titanic demands on the flower industry. Only a worldwide network of growers and shippers can accommodate our modern demand for flowers—orchids come from Singapore; tropical flowers from

Hawaii; roses from Ecuador; callas from New Zealand; and lily of the valley from Holland.

Recalling Heady Scents

Flowers evoke emotion and memory. We love them because they seduce our senses. Specific flowers are labeled as pure, innocent, stately, decadent, erotic, or even whimsical. Some blooms are miniscule and unassuming, while others are luscious and boisterous.

Personally, the heady fragrance of lilac wafting on evening breezes takes me back to those golden college days when I lived and loved life on Lilac Lane and further back to those carefree childhood days when my grandmother and I stuffed butterscotch candies and lilac into ribbon-laced May cones to hang on neighborhood doors. I'm certain that you have fond, flower-related memories of your own.

I simply adore flowers—I always have. I find it difficult to imagine a world without them—without their images, fragrances, or colors that inspire. I am delighted to offer you this book filled with photographs of vignettes and

A

B

C

D

E

G

F

H

wonderful flowers for eight special occasions. I encourage you to plan your next celebration with flowers in mind, and ask that you try the very doable ideas and techniques I have outlined in the following chapters.

What You Will Need

All of the projects in this book were planned with you, the reader, in mind. With very little effort, everyone can get their hands on the necessary ingredients.

The containers in this book are common ones—ceramic pots, simple glass vases, baskets, bowls, family silver, tea cups, and wooden salad bowls. Always begin with containers and props that you have on hand, or containers you can borrow from your sister or best friend. You can always supplement them with similar containers found

at thrift shops or local discount stores for very little money.

Floral supply items like floral foam, garden snips, hot glue, moss, Styrofoam, tape, wire, and wired picks are standard items that can be found at local craft stores or in the craft sections of discount stores. Fabrics and ribbons are available at craft stores or sewing centers.

Some things you will need:
• Containers (Photos A and B)
• Floral foam (Photo C)
• Floral tape (Photo D)
• Garden snips and scissors (Photo E)
• Hot glue gun and glue sticks (Photo F)
• Hot glue pan and glue pellets (Photo G)
• Moss (Photo H)
• Styrofoam balls (Photo I)
• Wired floral picks (Photo J)

Fruits, vegetables, and flowers can be purchased at the supermarket, local farmer's market, or in the produce department of warehouse stores. All of the projects in this book have been designed to use the more common flowers that can be purchased locally. Whenever possible, use flowers and produce from your own (or a friend's) yard and garden. There is nothing quite like a freshly cut garden rose or a plump home-grown hydrangea blossom. Plants can be pur-chased from local nurseries or home and garden centers. Keep in mind that being resourceful is the secret to creating a great look on a budget.

What You Will Learn

Most people are intimidated by the prospect of having to figure out how to successfully put flowers into a container so that they stay put and look good. Have no fear! There are numer-ous tricks of the trade that flower people use to control flowers and coddle them into containers. Anyone can learn these tricks—I'll show you how.

I will also show you alternative, less obvious ways of using flowers that will require you to learn a few simple techniques that I'm certain you will be able to master easily. The other techniques you will learn include hot gluing

flowers to surfaces, stringing flowers, and simply floating flowers.

Once your flower projects are completed there are ways to display them that will allow the flowers to shine. I'll show you how to display the flowers and how to team them up with fruit, vegetables, candles, and other props—upping the excitement with little additional effort.

Flowers do not mind being the center of attention in the middle of a table at a party but they also like to show up in less obvious places—in the salad, on the front door, on the back of a chair, or hanging from a garden hook.

A note about using a hot glue pan: Hot glue should be used at a medium temperature. At high heat, the glue smokes a bit and becomes so liquid that it slides off of the surfaces you are gluing. The temperature is right when you can dip your flower, leaf, or berry in the glue and there is a slight impression left in the glue pan. The glue will remain on your flower, leaf, or berry and will carry a little thread of glue as you pull it up out of the pan (Photos A, B, and C).

Come on—let's plan a party and do some flowers!

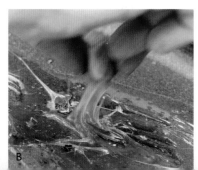

A   B   C

"In joy or sadness,

flowers are our constant friends.

We eat, drink, sing, dance,

and flirt with them."

—Kokuzo Okakura, THE BOOK OF TEA

Chapter 1

A Birthday Celebration

Far be it from us to allow a birthday to go by in an ordinary fashion. Birthdays are important markers in our lives. We experience the "terrible 2s," we go to kindergarten at age 5, we become adults at 18, we become middle age at 40, and we collect social security at 65. It is only natural that we celebrate "our" day with enthusiasm.

The birthday celebration has its own long-lived set of traditions—ice cream and cake with candles, a song, and presents. But a birthday party is much more fun when there are special activities planned around the people, places, and things that are nearest and dearest to the heart of the guest of honor.

Our birthday party celebrates a true girlie girl who simply adores the color pink. Her mom is the hostess and the guests are her best girl friends and their mothers. The invitation requests that mothers and daughters come dressed casually in pink or lavender clothes— the colors of the day—preferable in a floral pattern of some kind.

How perfect would it be if our location were profuse with cherry trees in full glorious pink blooms? Instead, we have transformed a simple backyard for the garden party. Trees are decked out in pink and lavender wind socks made of ribbons and blossoms. Embellished garden hooks heavy with flowering baskets are stationed at points of interest. The refreshment table holds a special cake display and garden urns that serve as a punch bowl and ice cream dish.

To keep little hands busy and guests happy, there are activity tables where mothers and daughters can create their own centerpieces using cut flowers, bird's nests, bugs, bees, and butterflies.

(Opposite) Layers of soft fabrics and a proliferation of pink flowers turn this ordinary backyard into a birthday wonderland.

Ribbon Windsock

What you will need

- ¹/₂"-wide lavender ribbon, 40 yards
- ¹/₂"-wide pink ribbon, 40 yards
- 7" diameter embroidery hoop, plastic or wood
- Flower heads, 2" across (optional)
- Hot glue gun
- Scissors

What you will do

1. Plug in the hot glue gun.
2. Precut the ribbons to 8' lengths.
3. Using a slipknot, add the 8' ribbons to the hoop.

To make a slipknot:

A. Find the middle of the length of ribbon.
B. Fold the ribbon at this point, causing a loop.
C. Bring the loop up and over the outer edge of the hoop, then down toward the center of the hoop.
D. Bring the two cut ends of the ribbon up through the loop together and pull until the loop tightens around the embroidery hoop.

4. Continue adding ribbons side by side until the surface of the ring is completely covered.
5. Cut four 4' lengths of ribbon. These are the hangers for your windsock.
6. At the four opposite sides of the hoop, attach one of the 4' ribbons with hot glue to the inner side of hoop. When glue is set, pull the loose ends of the ribbon ties together and knot them.
7. If desired, use hot glue to embellish the finished ring with flower heads.
8. Hang windsock from branches using ribbon or wire.

BLOOMING IDEA

A Little Tenderness

Some of us have hands more calloused than others. If you have problems with hot glue, choose a lower temperature glue gun and keep a small bowl of cold water close by to dip your fingers in if you get glue on them. The water is very soothing. Just remember to keep the water away from anything electrical.

(Opposite) Our whimsical windsocks add color and a festive flair to the day's celebration. (Above right, top and bottom) Pretty shades of pink define a celebration that's both pretty and fun.

Embellished Garden Hook

What you will need

- Garden hook
- Hanging basket with primarily pink flowers
- Pink satin ribbon, 2" wide x 5' long
- Scissors

What you will do

1. Decide where the hanging basket will be located.
2. Push the garden hook down into the soil at the desired location. Make sure to push down far enough into soil so it won't tip over.
3. Find the middle of the 5' piece of ribbon and tie it onto the upper part of the garden hook where it curves (Photo A).
4. Begin a series of lacing motions, tying a half-knot each time the ribbon comes back to the top of the hook (Photo B). The spacing of the half knots is up to you (Photos C). When you feel you have laced enough area, finish it off with a long looping bow (Photo D).
5. Finish off the ends of the ribbon with a nice clean cut.
6. Hang the basket on the hook and finish it with additional ribbon if you like.

BLOOMING IDEA

Just Hanging Around

In lieu of the planted basket, why not plump up a pretty little pink backpack with paper, tuck in some potted flowering plants, and slip it over the garden hook? Perhaps a charming hand-painted birdhouse hung on the garden hook with satin ribbons is just what your setting calls for. If your guest of honor is a miniature athlete, consider using your garden hook as a shoe tree by hanging pink ballet shoes, ice skates, or sneakers. Of course each shoe must have a nosegay of flowers tucked inside.

(Opposite) Floral baskets can be purchased or made at home. If you do decide to make your own, do them well ahead so they will be lush and full by party time. Line your wire basket with damp sheet moss and firmly tamp fresh potting soil around all of your plants.

SETTING AN ACTIVITY TABLE

No one goes home from this party lackluster or empty handed. Activity tables filled with all sorts of lovely accoutrements await party guests. There are freshly baked sugar cookies to be decorated, gilded picture frames to be embellished, sparkling beaded bracelets to be strung, and nicely scented centerpieces to be assembled.

What child has not picked dandelion blooms or wildflowers to take home to mom? Now mother and child can compose floral centerpieces together from the collection of flowers and garden-themed items found on this specially designed activity table. Everything is at the ready and everything is child friendly. The containers are prepared, the flowers and greens have been cut and conditioned in water, the necessary tools are present, and the fun final touches are waiting patiently in white baskets to be tucked in and among the flowers.

A friend of the hostess will be stationed at the table. She is an avid gardener and she will put together some simple arrangements of her own and will also assist the party guests if they so desire. She will be there with hand towels and little packing boxes when the centerpieces are complete.

(Above) Wide, open spaces and protected work surfaces are pretty—and practical. Colored vinyl sheeting can be purchased at floral supply stores.

(Opposite) This make-your-own centerpiece station is sure to keep little hands busy. Common easy-to-find flowers and embellishments ensure that all this beauty can be had on a budget.

Make-Your-Own Centerpiece Station

What you will need

- 8' table
- Bucket of water
- Children's scissors (for the girls)
- Cut greens (ivy, camellia, lemon leaf, or anything from your yard; keep in water bucket)
- Embellishments, birds, nests, bees, bugs, and butterflies (Photos A and B)
- Floral foam, 1 block for every 3 pots
- Fresh-cut flowers in water, 6 per person (gerbera daisies, daisy mums, and carnations are durable and easy for children to handle)
- Garden snips or sharp knife (for the moms)
- Little pots or fancy containers, 1 per guest (Photo C)
- Long, flat spatula
- Small wired picks
- Table covering (easy to clean)

What you will do

1. Make a sample centerpiece to inspire the budding artists who will then create their own arrangements.

(continued on page 24)

BLOOMING IDEA

Nature's Own

Birds, bees, and bugs can be found at the nearest craft store but feel free to include "found" objects on this garden table. Spill out some smooth river rocks, clumps of moss, bits of interesting driftwood, flower bulbs, feathers, or even mushrooms from the grocery store. The avid gardener who will be assisting at the table can come armed with her glue gun and some extra picks. Every creation should be fun to create and keep, and have its own charm. Let your guests know that there is no right or wrong way to put the flower arrangements together—just *their* way.

(Opposite) Our little centerpiece is easy to create. Make sure to have one assembled ahead of time to inspire the budding artists at the party.

(continued from page 23)

2. Submerge each block of floral foam in the bucket of water. Leave in the water until bubbles no longer rise to the surface.

3. Using a flat spatula, cut each block into three equal parts.

4. Stand the foam blocks on their ends and slice off a small piece of each corner. The blocks should then fit nicely into the containers. If the blocks of foam rise above the lip of the containers more than 1", slice off the excess foam. Your containers are now ready for flowers and other embellishments.

5. Cut the stems of the flowers with garden snips and put them in containers of tepid water. Do the same with bits and pieces of greens, making sure they are easy for children to handle.

6. Wrap wire on the picks around the legs of the bugs and birds and around the wire on the butterflies. Run the wires through the mesh of nests and twist until the nests rest securely on the picks.

BLOOMING IDEA

Waterproof Containers

Most pots made for plants are designed with holes in the bottom so that excess water can drain away. I chose the decorative blue and white pots featured in this project because they were nice and also on sale for 50 percent off. In order to adapt them for use as containers for cut flowers they must first be lined with something waterproof so that wet floral foam can be put in them to hold the flower stems. I chose to use a double layer of heavy plastic sheeting that I got in a large roll at the hardware store. Half-pound plastic containers (those used for macaroni and cheese or potato salad) are a good size. Plastic butter tubs and cottage cheese containers also work as liners. Large plastic drinking cups cut down a bit are also good. I suggest that you take a few different liners to the garden center or discount store and try them in various pots until you find the combination that suits you and your wallet.

(Opposite) With leftover flowers from the children's activity table, we created a tussie mussie especially for the birthday girl.

(From top) Embellishments such as tiny bird's nests and ladybug picks can be found at crafts and floral supply stores; carnations are long-lasting, hearty flowers that can withstand the handling of little hands.

Floral Birthday Cake Stand

What you will need

- 1 yard fabric
- 12"- to 18"-diameter hat box
- Flower heads
- Hot glue gun
- Pins
- Roll of brown packaging paper or freezer paper
- Round pre-cut particle board
- Scissors
- Soft measuring tape
- Spray adhesive

What you will do

1. Remove the hat box lid because you won't need it.
2. Measure the height and circumference of the box and add 2" to each measurement. Transpose those measurements to brown paper to make a pattern.
3. Put the particle board round down on a large piece of brown paper. Cut around the particle board, leaving a generous 5" margin all the way around. This makes your second pattern.
4. Pin the two patterns to your fabric and cut them out.
5. Spray glue onto backside of the fabric.
6. Lay the hat box on its side on the fabric, leaving a 1" margin of fabric at the top and a 1" margin of fabric at the bottom. With your clean fingers or a soft cloth, smooth the glued fabric into place a little bit at a time, until the side of the hat box is covered. Tuck under the excess at the end to make a nice finish. Secure the end with hot glue.
7. The excess 1" on the top and bottom are then folded neatly over the edges of the box. Secure with hot glue.
8. Repeat this process for the pre-cut particle board round. The excess fabric on this piece will need to be eased over the edges carefully to ensure a nice uniform look.
9. Hot glue the fabric covered round to the bottom of the covered hat box.
10. Hot glue embellishments onto the cake stand. Remember, the cake stand should enhance—not take attention away from—the cake.

(Opposite) A beautiful cake stand makes a simple cake look extraordinary, and somehow more delicious! Ours echoes all of the design elements of the day— we've used the same ribbons and flowers on the cake stand (above) found at the centerpiece station and in the windsocks.

BLOOMING IDEA

Finding the Right Piece

Craft stores often have round and square papier-mâché boxes with lids that work very well for the cake stand project. Ideally, the size of the box should be smaller than the size of your cake. Home improvement centers have pre-cut round particle boards. Choose a size at least 3" to 4" larger than the circumference of your cake.

CAKE ON DISPLAY

Often much thought and effort goes into decorating a cake or selecting a special cake from a bakery and just as much thought and effort should go into displaying the special cake.

Britney Spears Federline's wedding cake was displayed on a floral cake stand (pictured at right). Apparently, Sam Godfrey of Perfect Endings in Napa Valley (another designer to the stars) boxed and shipped Britney's cake on ice, sending it by express delivery to arrive the day before the wedding in Los Angeles.

Britney wanted something simple and traditional so she chose a two-tiered scalloped layered white chocolate butter cake with white chocolate ganache. The cake was decorated with handmade roses and edible pearls. The cake was small and delicate and displayed on a 36" round table. The white rose-covered hat box we created was the perfectly understated lift that the glorious cake needed and deserved. Just under 500 white Eskimo roses pavé the surface of the box, adding drama and interest.

(Above) Much effort goes into decorating a cake, yet seldom do we think about overdoing it. Adding fresh flowers does just that.

(Opposite) Brittany Spears and Kevin Federline's wedding cake was displayed on a floral cake stand of white roses.

Chapter 2

An Anniversary Celebration

The milestone of a loving marriage is a wonderful occasion to celebrate. Our party is a wine tasting in honor of a couple celebrating their 10th wedding anniversary. The couple spent their honeymoon in Tuscany and they cherish memories of the vineyards, wine, and the warm people they met. The guest list is small and includes couples who are the best of friends.

We bring Tuscany home by creating an atmosphere that echoes the Italian countryside. To welcome guests, the front door is adorned with an Italian-inspired wire basket of fruit and flowers that gives a hint as to what waits beyond.

An arbor or outdoor room would be a perfect setting, but any spacious room where an overhead grid of votive candles can be hung for the evening will work.

A heavy wood buffet table appointed with slabs of marble and hardwood piled high with cheeses, breads, fruits, and other delectables is centered under a shower of shimmering votives.

The colors of the evening are the colors of grapes—greens, amethyst, and merlot. And there must be candlelight, lots of candlelight, for ambience. To complete the picture, sparkling colored glass vases filled with gracious garden roses rise above the culinary offerings.

Be sure to set a small table for take-home gifts. Keep the table out of sight until just before your guests depart for the evening.

(Opposite) A table laden with flowers and candlelight ensures a celebration to remember. Simple flowers in a bold hue command attention. For added drama, use risers to vary the height of the centerpieces.

Fruit and Flower Door Basket

What you will need

- 20" x 20" piece of black felt
- Artificial grapes
- Branches of fall leaves, 2
- Bridal holders with floral foam, 2
- Chenille or pipe cleaners, 4
- Colored pencil with white lead
- Garden snips
- Hot glue gun
- Moss or fabric (optional)
- Red roses, 8
- Scissors
- Small bucket of water
- Small flat-backed wire or woven basket
- Small wooden picks with wires
- Styrofoam (optional)
- Wreath hanger

What you will do

1. Lay the basket, flat side down, on the felt and draw around it with the white pencil. Cut out the shape and hot glue it to the back of the basket. Trim any excess. This will protect your door from scratches.

2. If the basket has openwork like this one you will need to use moss or fabric behind the openwork to make it opaque. A piece of Styrofoam has also been added to make a false bottom, because the basket is so deep.

3. Plug in your glue gun and soak the bridal holders in a small bucket of water. Score the handles of the bridal holder with a heavy pair of garden snips; snap the handles off. Run a pipe cleaner thru the holes in the bridal holders and then wire them in place near the top of the basket. Hot glue the bridal holders to make certain they are very secure.

4. Wrap the wire on the small wooden picks to the stems of the grapes until they are secure on the picks. Secure the juncture with a little hot glue to keep everything together.

5. Push the ends of the picks into the bridal holders until the grapes dangle gracefully over the edge of the basket.

6. Snip the roses one at a time and tuck them in the wet foam of the bridal holder.

7. Use fall leaves or any other cut greens from your yard to fill noticeable spaces.

8. Position the wreath hanger on your door and add your finished basket.

BLOOMING IDEA

Pretty Hangers

If you wish to disguise an unattractive wreath hanger or simply dress up a plain one, apply spray paint or wrap pretty ribbon around it. If you do not mind a nail hole in your door, you will not need to use a wreath hanger.

(Opposite and above) Fresh grapes in both purple and green recall the abundance of Italy. Green moss beautifully hides the bridal holders that keep the flowers and grapes in place.

Glass Vases Filled with Roses

What you will need

- Floral adhesive tape, clear
- Green and amethyst glass vases, various shapes and sizes
- Knife or sharp garden snips
- Red roses, loose, 20
- Scissors
- Wispy greens or berries

What you will do

1. Tape a grid on top opening of wide-mouthed vases so that as you tuck in stems of roses, the stems stay put (see page 74).

2. Fill all the vases with tepid water.

3. Strip leaves from rose stems that will be submerged in vase. Keep a few leaves at the top because they are a vital part of the grace and charm of the flower—and the arrangement.

4. Before you put the roses in vases, hold a single rose up to the vase to determine where to cut the stem so that it settles into the vase nicely yet rises above it gracefully—about 3". Do this with each rose until you begin to know instinctively how long to make the roses for each vase. Continue adding roses to the vases until it looks like you've gone too far. Pull one out and call it finished.

BLOOMING IDEA

Happy Flowers Last Longer

To help blooms last longer, make sure that as you snip each rose, you put it in water right away. This prevents the cell structure in the stem from sealing itself off. When the stem is sealed off water cannot travel up to the bloom, which results in a shorter life for flowers.

(Top) Start your arrangement with the center flower. Be sure it stands taller than all of the others.

(Above) Rather than a vase full of long-stem flowers, top the vase with an arrangement of roses cut very short and tucked in a plastic ring of floral foam. This is a great way to utilize flowers with broken stems.

(Opposite) The beauty of the roses takes center stage when blooms are displayed in simple glass vases.

PLEASE TOSS THESE PETALS
AFTER BRIT & KEVIN'S KISS
AND WISH FOR THEM
YEARS AND YEARS OF HAPPINESS!!

A CELEBRITY'S BIG DAY

Britney Spears and Kevin Federline asked their wedding planner, Alyson Fox, to arrange an informal, Southern-inspired buffet of finger foods. Fried chicken, Louisiana crab cakes, and spare ribs were featured.

Equally hearty flower arrangements of Black Magic roses, red Classy roses, and hot pink Yves Piaget roses in silver punctuated the setting. Furniture had been removed from this dining room so that guests could move about more easily but the tall, lovely arrangements allowed the open and empty space to remain warm and friendly while also allowing for easy access to all the special dishes.

Imagine this same table with every item low to the table and you will understand more fully the impact of height. Layering is not only more visually stimulating but it actually helps to create space for additional items.

Food and flowers are fine companions. Flowers have always enhanced the finest of laid tables. It is important to remember that when you entertain, be sure to make every attempt to tantalize all five senses.

(Above) Cones are a timeless tradition celebrated by each new generation. Britney Spears and Kevin Federline gave guests these gift cones filled with red rose petals at their wedding.

(Opposite) When putting together the tables at Britney Spears and Kevin Federline's wedding and reception, we made the most of the table space by using risers.

Arrangement in Iron Urn

What you will need

- 4" x 4" piece of chicken wire
- Block of floral foam, I
- Garden snips
- Hot glue gun
- Hydrangea, 3-4 full blooms
- Iron urn
- Papier-mâché liner, size 201
- Red roses, 48
- Sharp knife or cake spatula
- Sheet moss
- Waterproof floral tape, green

What you will do

1. Thoroughly soak the block of floral foam.
2. Stand the block of floral foam on its side. Cut in half with a wide cake spatula or knife and place in liner. Very slightly, bevel top edges of floral foam. Trim off the corners with a wide cake spatula or knife. The foam should rise I" above the surface of the liner. Using floral tape, go across the wet foam and clear around the papier-mache liner.
3. Hot glue covering of sheet moss onto liner and slide into urn.
4. Make an X cut at end of each hydrangea and place them around edge of liner, like a collar.
5. Hold a stem of rose up to the urn and decide at what length it looks best in proportion to the urn. Cut stems one at a time, allowing an additional 3" of stem to go down into the foam. Start in the middle of the liner and as you put in each flower, aim the stem toward the center of the foam like branches on the trunk of a tree.
6. Hot glue moss to cover edges of liner.

(Opposite) The linear structure of the brown metal urn echoes the linear repetition of brown ribbons encasing the hanging votives. (Above right, top and bottom) Fresh fruit and flowers are natural accompaniments to each other.

BLOOMING IDEA
Daily Watering

Ideally flowers are open and in the height of their glory the day of your party. If you want to enjoy them for a few days more be certain to add water. Some flowers, like roses, drink generous amounts of water. Manageable vases of flowers can be placed in a large sink where you can carefully allow a stream of water from the faucet to flow past the edge of the vase, flushing out the stale water and gradually replacing it with fresh water. Flowers arranged in floral foam must be watered differently and more delicately. A turkey baster filled with water fits into small spaces more easily. If it is difficult to see the existing water level in an opaque container test it with your finger and add water until you know by touch that the water is near the top.

(Above) Wooden boxes or crates can be found at crafts stores. They can either be left in their natural state (top), for a more rustic look, or they may be covered with a beautiful silk for a more formal affair (bottom).

BLOOMING IDEA

Reflexing Your Rose

A single red rose is stunning in any setting. We've laid them at various places on the table simply because they are beautiful.

To achieve a full-bloom look (opposite), you will need to begin with a rose that is at least half-way open. (Photo A) Starting with the outermost petals of the rose (Photo B), use your thumb and forefinger to encourage the petals to roll outward. This is called reflexing, and it does take a gentle touch. Continue turning the petals out until your rose has a nice full look (Photo C).

GETTING A RISE

The difference between a homespun presentation and an elegant affair really is in the details. Risers give much-needed height variances for displaying flowers and food. Covered risers become part of the presentation and are so easy to make.

Most anything can be called into service as a riser. Caterers use milk crates and heavy wooden storage boxes used for storing chafing dishes and coffee service. The homemaker can use large bowls or kettles and pots turned upside down. Large, clean terra-cotta pots and bowls also can be used as long as they have some weight and sit firmly on the table with a relatively broad base.

Simply disguise your risers by draping them with coordinating linens. Puddle any excess fabric with a bit of flair and thought. Coordinating tablecloths are ideal, but to keep costs down, don't hesitate to buy some yardage and use it the same way, making certain that raw edges are tucked under if you decide not to hem the fabric. (I've been known to hot glue or hand stitch a few hems in my time.)

If you want a more stylishly clean and finished look to your table, cover boxes like the boxes we covered for the anniversary party. Begin with a collection of sturdy boxes and fabric that works with the décor of your party. Faux leather, suede, and silk dupioni are all effective fabric finishes. Place the box, open side up, on the fabric and cut a piece of fabric a couple of inches larger than the circumference of the box. Wrap the box as if you were wrapping a gift. Pull two opposing sides of fabric up tightly and smoothly and secure them to the inside of the box with hot glue.

Treat the other two sides as you would a gift, tucking in the corners of the fabric, pulling the flap up, and securing the flap with hot glue to the inside of the box.

A

B

C

D

Hanging Votives with Colored Water

What you will need

- ³/₈" ribbon for each bowl, 4'
- Floral adhesive tape, clear
- Food coloring, green and yellow
- Glass rose bowls, 8-10
- Hot glue gun
- Pitcher of water
- Scissors
- Small, clean pebbles
- Votive candles, 8-10
- Votive cups, 8-10

What you will do

1. Cut the ribbon into 2' lengths.
2. Turn each bowl over, open end down. Find the middle of one length of ribbon and place it in the glue. Add a second dab of glue and place another ribbon in it, forming an X on the bottom of the glass.
3. Turn the bowl right side up and pull the ribbon lengths up around the curves of the bowl—
   this will form a cradle of ribbon. Run a line of floral adhesive tape around the top of the bowl to hold the ribbons in place. Bring all the ribbon ends together and knot them.
4. Put a votive cup filled with a few pebbles and votive wax in each rose bowl.
5. Fill a clear pitcher with water. To the water add 4-5 drops of yellow food coloring. Stir, then add 1 drop of green.
6. Hang rose bowls from chandelier or rack. Trim ribbons as needed (Photo A).
7. Add a bit of colored water to each rose bowl (Photo B).
8. Light votives (Photo C) and enjoy (Photo D) the romantic ambience.

BLOOMING IDEA

For Safety's Sake

Make sure to do a trial run with one of the votive holders before hanging.

Thinner glass may break from the heat of the candle. Use heat-tempered

glass to ensure everyone's safety.

(Opposite) These eye-catching votives add drama and romance to our celebration.
To help keep the hanging light in balance, be sure to evenly counter the weight of
the votives when tying them around your grid or candelabrum.

CREATING A ROMANTIC HIDEAWAY

Britney Spears and Kevin Federline had originally planned to be married at a resort in Santa Barbara, California in the company of family and hundreds of friends. The mother-daughter wedding planning team of Levine-Fox Events had begun to quietly finalize all of the endless details, but alas the media caught wind of a celebrity wedding in the making and joy-filled planning turned to apprehension.

Under the guise of an engagement party, the two lovebirds were secretly married at a home in a Los Angeles suburb in the company of a handful of family and friends instead. The living and dining rooms of the home were cleared of furniture and miles upon miles of ivory fabric transformed the space and the quaintly tented back patio into a romantic hideaway.

A rose-encrusted double arch filled the picture window of the home but prying eyes could not see beyond the draping. Drapery was pulled back at interior doorways with wide floral cuffs made of fabric-covered chicken wire with pavé roses and hydrangea.

The flowered garland draped on the living room fireplace also began as a chicken wire form. It defines a mantel lined with silver candle stands, glass, and pillar candles. Small rose nosegays are tucked in here and there. Twin topiaries heavily laden with antique hydrangea and deep red and pink roses flank the fireplace and scrumptious mounds of rose petals with edges feathered out add that final delicious touch.

After the ceremony the guests were treated to the buffet in the dining room and music and cocktails in the outdoor tent enclosing the patio.

(Above) For Britney Spears Federline's wedding, fabric draping was pulled back with floral cuffs to create a doorway into the candlelit ceremony area. A simple white fireplace was transformed with layers upon layers of roses and candles.

INSPIRATION FROM KATE BECKINSALE

To create a special place for the children at Kate Beckinsale's wedding, event planner Mindy Weiss transformed a tented area on the lawn with billowy pink fabric, a serpentine table and stools just the right height for small guests. The stools were dressed in pink skirts and pink boas were added for flair. The center of the table was lined with flowers in a child-friendly palette of colors. The arrangements were kept low, so young friends could easily see over them.

Wine Case Favors

What you will need

- ¹/₂ yard ribbon per wine case
- Bottle of wine, 1 per guest
- Fresh ivy leaves, small flower blossoms, berry sprigs
- Hot glue gun
- Pen
- Small cluster of artificial grapes per wine case
- Small gift card, 1 per guest
- Wine case with cord, 1 per guest

What you will do

1. Put a bottle of wine in each wine case and pull up the cord handle firmly.
2. Knot ribbon tightly around one end of the cord handle, adding a tiny dab of hot glue first.
3. Write a short sentiment on the gift card (Photo A).
4. Hot glue small cluster of grapes, flower blossoms, fresh leaves, and small sprigs of berries to top of wine case (Photo B).
5. Group wine cases on table (Photo C).
6. Adorn table with fresh blossoms and artificial grapes.

(Opposite) A tabletop overflowing with rose petals keeps the romance going until the party's last dance. The wine case favors are a nice parting touch.

Chapter 3

A Reunion Celebration

It has been said that once you leave home you can never truly go back. Oh, but what great fun and how humbling it is to revisit familiar people, places, and happenings. School mates, military personnel, business associates, girlfriends, and, of course, family members all have reunions. The longer the absence and the closer the relationship of friends or family the more powerful the coming together—lost time simply melts away.

Reunions connote a certain coziness, much like the early days of the fall season. Plan to hold your gathering while the weather is still amicable for everyone.

The theme should definitely have something to do with comfort and abundance. There is no place like a home for the gathering—especially if the home has some wonderful spaces such as a great hearth with lots of firewood for the evening.

To put yourself in the decorating mood, put a saucepan filled half way with water on the stove, turn the burner on low, and throw in some pieces of apple, a few cloves, and some cinnamon and wait for the smells of the fall season to get you up, motivated, and inspired.

Deck out the fireplace mantel with baskets overflowing with long-lasting squash, gourds, and sunflowers. Dress a table with cinnamon- and apple-scented candles surrounded by jewel-like textures. Every nook and corner of the house should be inviting.

The colors favored by fall are mossy greens, golds, oranges, and rusts.

(Opposite) Welcome fall and those you love with this cozy fireside tableau. Everything found in the arrangements can be gathered from your local grocery store, nursery, and floral supply store.

Tangerine Topiary Tree

What you will need

- 3/8" wood screws, 8
- 1/2" plumbing phalanges, 2
- 1/2" threaded lead pipe, 36" long
- 12" particle board rounds, 2
- 25-pound bag of plaster
- Branches with berries
- Bucket or large pot
- Curly willow
- Fall or magnolia leaves
- Floral wire
- Hot glue and glue pan
- Serrated knife
- Styrofoam ball, 10" diameter
- Tangerines or oranges, 4-6 bags
- Wooden picks

What you will do

1. Screw one plumbing phalange to the center of one round particle board.
2. Screw the second phalange to the center of the second round particle board.
3. Shape your topiary stand by screwing each of the two ends of threaded pipe into one of the phalanges. Your topiary stand is ready to sink into plaster to create a strong base to hold the weight of the tangerines.
4. Place one end of the base into a bucket or large pot. Prepare the plaster according to manufacturer's directions. Pour the prepared plaster mixture into the bucket or pot (if you are using a bucket, fill only half way). Allow plaster to harden.

(continued on page 52)

(Opposite and above) Beautiful and unique, the tangerine topiary fills the room with fragrance.

(continued from page 51)

5. Using a serrated knife, cut off one-third of the Styrofoam ball. Discard the small piece.

6. Melt hot glue in glue pan; dribble a good amount of hot glue onto the flat surface of the larger dome of Styrofoam. Lay the Styrofoam on the top particle board round. The topiary is now ready for embellishment.

7. Push a wooden pick into each orange or tangerine.

8. While cupping the fruit in your hand, push the other end of the pick into the Styrofoam. Begin at the top center and work in concentric circles. Make sure to place fruit as close together as possible. Completely cover the dome with fruit.

9. To complete the top of the topiary dome, dip the stem ends of fall leaves into hot glue and tuck them into spaces between oranges. Add berries if desired.

10. Cover the bottom side of the dome with fall or magnolia leaves. Apply hot glue to the stems and apply to bottom side of dome. Overlap and repeat until covered.

11. Place the topiary in a decorative pot or basket.

12. To disguise the pipe, place branches along the side of the pipe (Photo A) and wire into place. Add curly willow and wire into place.

13. Cover the exposed plaster with leaves or moss, or wedge wet floral foam in the container and arrange magnolia leaves in the foam (Photo B).

BLOOMING IDEA

Tantalizing Topiaries

This topiary could just as easily have been made with green apples or red pears. The instructions remain the same. The topiary could also have been a cone shape instead of a dome. I simply decided to repeat the shape of the heavy ceramic bowl that I chose to put my topiary in.

(Opposite) This tall topiary brings drama to the front of this fireplace, while the candles lend ambiance.

(Above) Baskets of varying heights are filled with the bounty of the fall season.
Their warm colors echo those of the painting above, tying the look all together.

FALL BEAUTIES

What other flower could possibly be as heart-warming as the sunflower? Van Gogh recognized and immortalized its wonderful qualities in many of his paintings.

This fine fellow is known for always turning its face to the sun. Several varieties keep good company here—the shaggy yellow one without the distinctive brown center is called a "teddy bear."

Adding a few fall leaves takes sunflowers from being popular summer flowers to being fall beauties.

When you shop for fresh produce for your displays at home, look for new varieties of squash and pumpkins. Many of today's selections are actually old varieties called heirlooms grown from resurrected seeds. They often have unusual coloration and striations. If the skin is not broken or bruised, the fruit will easily last the whole fall season, making the arrangement a long-lasting tribute to fall.

I do realize that tangerines are not generally thought of as part of the fall harvest but their color and size were perfect for this project. Don't be afraid of thinking outside the box. Grab some hearty, but somewhat small, fruit from the season's harvest and get busy making your own topiary.

Fireplace Mantel

What you will need

- 2" green Styrofoam sheet
- Baskets, 5-6 medium-sized of similar shape, color, or both
- Branches
- Cake spatula or knife
- Floral foam, 3 blocks
- Florist's polyfoil or plastic sheeting
- Garden snips
- Pumpkins, gourds, squash
- Sunflowers, 30

What you will do

1. Line your tallest basket with florist's polyfoil or cut a double layer of plastic sheeting to fit generously down into the basket.

2. Thoroughly soak two blocks of floral foam in water.

3. Stand the blocks of floral foam on their sides and trim off the corners with a wide cake spatula or knife. Place the floral foam blocks in the liner. Don't force them; feel free to shave more of the foam off so they fit tightly but nicely. The foam should rise 2" above the surface of the basket. If the foam is too short, simply soak your third piece of foam and cut off a piece that will fit in the basket underneath the two blocks of foam in order to lift them higher.

4. Hold a stem of sunflowers up to the basket and decide at what length they look best in proportion to the basket. I like them to sit low and plumped together for this project. Cut stems one at a time, allowing an additional 3" of stem to go down into the foam. Start in the middle of the basket, and as you put in each flower, aim the stem toward the center of the basket, like branches on the trunk of a tree. This way the flowers will fan out nicely instead of standing up like soldiers.

5. Fill empty spaces with short branches of leaves from your yard. Place the basket on the mantel just a little off-center (this is one of the tricks to make something more eye-catching). Begin placing the other baskets of vegetables along the mantel, turning some of them on their sides. (This will allow squash and gourds to spill out.)

6. To elevate vegetables in baskets, cut pieces of Styrofoam to fit snugly in the baskets. Layer the Styrofoam until it is high enough to make a good platform for gourds.

7. Position all the baskets, and when you are happy with the way they look, add the remaining pumpkins, gourds, and squash. Finish with a few branches of leaves or berries.

(Above) If you don't have leaves in fall colors readily available, dried or silk variations can be found at floral and craft stores.

Cluster of Decorated Candles

What you will need

- Floral clay
- Mixed nuts in shell, 2 pounds
- Pillar candles, various sizes, colors, and fragrances
- Small oranges, 3
- Whole cloves
- Wooden tray

What you will do

1. Arrange your selection of candles on the tray, shifting them around until you get a pleasing look from all angles.
2. Lift each candle, one at a time, and put a dollop of floral clay on the bottom of the candle. Return the candle to its position on the tray and press into place. Repeat this procedure with each candle.
3. Spill the nuts into the tray and allow them to rest where they will (Photo A).
4. Create a simple pattern in cloves on one or two of the oranges, then add all of the oranges to the tray, clustering at least two of them together (Photo B).
5. Snip the candle wicks a bit if necessary and light them for a trial run.

A

B

BLOOMING IDEA

Melting Down

Eventually melted candle wax will drip down into your tray.

To protect the tray, be sure to line it with something firm and

unobtrusive, perhaps a piece of clear acetate or a piece of cork

you can temporarily fasten into place and then discard. The

more closely the candles are placed to each other the more

heat they will generate and the more likely the liquid wax will

escape the candle and run into your tray.

(Opposite) When your mantel holds nature's bounty, don't run the risk of fire by lighting low-laying candles. Instead, create a tray of candles to occupy the main table in the room.

Chapter 4

A Wedding Celebration

My friend, Kitty Bartholomew, who is a television personality and author extraordinaire of home decorating books, asked me to collaborate with her on her daughter Brooke's wedding. Brooke is a classic beauty with simple but refined taste.

Her preferences are not unlike those of her mother. Kitty, with Brooke's blessing, decided to use floral still-life paintings by the old Flemish masters as the inspiration for the flowers that would adorn the guest tables for the wedding celebration following the ceremony.

A wonderful mixture of blue and white porcelain vases served as the vessels that would hold graceful red tulips, antique blue hydrangea, and berries and vines reminiscent of the flowers and textures in the paintings. Companion pieces included candles and brass candlesticks, old books, and brass bowls spilling over with lovely plump fruit for that Old World flavor.

The reception decor was the crescendo of color and texture on this wedding day. The lawn ceremony was simply styled—only the red carpet down the aisle hinted at the color to come.

Cocktails were served on the veranda at dusk. Creamy white was the only color in attendance, however, the elements of fruit and candlelight made their initial appearance. A lemon topiary and votive candles graced the bar and clusters of towering glass cylinders with pillar candles punctuated the full sweep of the veranda high above the rolling lawn.

As the French doors of the grand ballroom were thrown open and the guest tables came into view, all of the design elements of the day came together in an explosion of color, texture, and candlelight.

(Opposite) The floral arrangements in this grand ballroom echo an Old World Flemish still-life painting. Every corner of the room—from the mantel to the cake stand—receives special attention in the form of flowers.

DEFINED BY OLD TRADITIONS

Once the look of the centerpiece was decided, all of the other floral embellishment decisions fell right into place. The same flowers, blue and white patterns, and metal surfaces would reappear in surprising new applications.

The size of the guest list ruled out an intimate home wedding. A warm, golden-toned ballroom overlooking a lovely veranda and rolling green lawns high above the Pacific Ocean became the venue of choice.

Weddings are a celebration defined by many old traditions with obscure beginnings that require the company of flowers. The ceremonial altar and aisle are often profuse with flowers. In contrast, we played down the flower aspect in the ceremony and allowed Brooke and her bridesmaids to be the true flowers of the day. This allowed flowers to take on more significance in the celebration phase of this wedding.

Flowers showed up in the cocktail area, on the place card table, on the mantel and guest tables, and finally as sweet endings on the cake table. Any one of these flower projects is easy enough to emulate with the proper supplies and a few simple instructions. Give them a whirl—you will have success and you will feel quite accomplished.

(From top) Brooke gathered her bridesmaids and friends for a luncheon and floral arranging; the fun invitation asked guests to join the bride in creating arrangements for the wedding celebration and reception; each guest was presented with a work apron that read "Bridal Brigade."

BLOOMING IDEA

With a Little Help from Her Friends

A wedding, her wedding, is the most unique and intensely

emotional event in a young woman's life—it is important

that every aspect of the day be perfect. Brooke and Kitty

not only planned and personalized the wedding day very

carefully, they planned the day before the wedding as well.

Friends of the bride were invited to gather after the

rehearsal luncheon to help arrange flowers for the next

day's festivities. Everything needed for the day was provided,

including lessons in floral arranging. Group participation

is unique but why not? Weddings, because of their

poignant nature, provide wonderful bonding time.

Lemon Topiary

What you will need

- 2"-thick Styrofoam sheet
- 4" wooden picks with wire
- Black marker
- Bunches of berries
- Clippings of greens, like camellia leaves
- Container
- Hot glue gun
- Lemons or any other small citrus fruit
- Serrated bread knife
- Small white blooms, 2-3 (optional)

What you will do

1. Turn the container upside down on the Styrofoam sheet and draw around it with a black marker.

(continued on page 65)

(Opposite) Fabulous containers are available in copper and galvanized metal in a variety of shapes and sizes at your local crafts and hardware stores. (Above, clockwise from top left) Ideal ingredients for our low arrangement include radiant berries, green leaves, and fresh citrus.

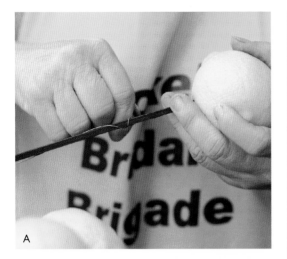

A

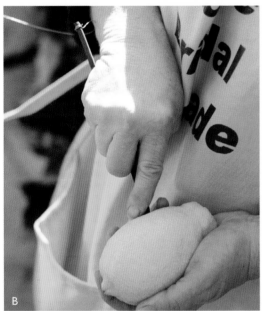

B

C

(Opposite) A standard topiary would require that picks be inserted into the ends of lemons so that when you finish there is a very uniform look to the whole piece. We chose to insert picks randomly instead, exposing some of the lovely coloring on the sides of the fruit.

(continued from page 63)

2. Using the serrated knife, cut out the Styrofoam shape, but be sure you cut well inside the black line so that the shape will fit into the container. If necessary, sand the edges of the shape with a scrap of Styrofoam until it slips into the container. Your container will probably need several layers of Styrofoam to create a surface level with the top of the container. Hot glue the layers together to create a firm base.

3. Begin the arrangement in the center of the Styrofoam. Push a wooden pick into the end of a lemon until it reaches the center (Photos A and B).

4. Cup the lemon in your hand with the exposed end of the pick between your fingers. Push the exposed pick into the Styrofoam, taking care to avoid pushing so hard that the stick comes through the opposite side of the fruit.

5. Repeat Step 4 again and again, working in a circular pattern around the center lemon. Place each successive lemon as close to its neighbor as space will allow (Photo C). (There are bound to be some gaps but the plan is to keep the gaps to a minimum and as small as possible.)

6. Continue until the surface of the Styrofoam is covered with fruit.

7. Fill in the gaps with clippings of glossy green leaves and hot glue. Camellia leaves are especially nice because they hold up and are reminiscent of the lemon's own leaves.

8. Tuck in 2-3 small white blooms like orange blossoms or stephanotis blooms, if desired.

BLOOMING IDEA

Topiary Tips

Estimate the amount of fruit you will need by holding one piece up to the opening of the container and visually estimating how many more will be required. It is better to overestimate—you can always make lemonade.

Also, choose a container with a low center of gravity so it doesn't tip over with the weight of the fruit. You can find copper or aluminum tubs at many kitchen and floral design stores.

Sitting Pretty Bench

What you will need

- Bench with a back
- Bucket of water
- Flats of ground cover, 2-3 (Photo A)
- Hot glue pan and glue
- Mood moss (Photo B)
- Plastic sheeting
- Popsicle stick
- Sharp knife
- Spray paint, your color choice

What you will do

1. Spray paint the bench and allow it to dry completely.
2. Cut a piece of plastic sheeting that just fits over the seat of the bench.
3. Carefully remove the ground cover from the flats so it stays in one piece (Photo C). If your bench is too narrow to accommodate the full flat, trim the excess with a knife.
4. Completely cover the surface of the bench with groundcover (Photo D).
5. Soak moss in water (Photo E). Squeeze excess water from moss, then apply hot glue to back of moss using a Popsicle stick (Photo F). Add moss to front edge of bench (Photo G).
6. Place completed bench in your space of choice (Photo H).

(Opposite) This bench commands attention, giving guests something to talk about as they collect their seat assignments prior to sitting down.

...Bob

Kem...

...Jason

Keyser, Mac :

Crane, Bryan : Brooke

...ft Eric

...bler.

Knight, David

...Eric

A

B

D

Pillows Talk

What you will need

- Fine-tip marker
- Flower heads
- Garden snips
- Hot glue pan or glue gun
- Inexpensive throw pillows in your color choice, 2
- Leaves

What you will do

1. Buy or gather the necessary flowers and leaves. Simply draw or trace your pattern of flowers (see tip box at right) on each of the pillows with a fine-tip marker.
2. Snip the flower heads and leaves off of their stems.
3. Apply a dab of glue to a leaf at its stem end and position it on the pillow (Photos A and B). Repeat this step with each leaf, but as you lay the leaf on the pillow overlap the previous leaf just enough to cover the spot where glue was put (Photo C). (The hot glue will burn a little spot and alter the color so this is our way of disguising that.)
4. Complete all of your leaf patterns.
5. Carefully touch the base of the flower head to the hot glue (Photo D) and put it in place on the pillow top. Hold the flower in place just a couple of seconds until the glue sets (Photo E) and the flower holds its position on its own (Photo F).

E

F

BLOOMING IDEA

As You Like It

The pillow project can be as simple or as complex as you wish to make it. Complex designs require more flowers and leaves. I suggest that you make a paper pattern of your pillow and draw a design on the pattern. Lay out a few flowers and leaves on it to estimate how many you will need to complete the design. Take the number and multiply by two if you are doing a second pillow.

(Opposite) These pretty pillows certainly dress up our place card bench, but they also could adorn your garden bench for any celebration.

THE GRANDEUR OF PAVÉ

The photographs on these two pages are perfect examples of two kinds of pavé surfaces. I've always assumed that the word pavé is a fancified version of the words "to pave" (to cover the surface of, as in to pave the road with asphalt). I've yet to be told differently.

The uniform layers of roses on the opposite page were made by hot gluing rose heads, one at a time, to precut Styrofoam sheets edged with double-faced satin ribbon. The roses could also have been inserted into white trays filled with wet floral foam so that they would last for several days.

Generally, because of time constraints, labor-intensive party work is designed to be beautiful just for the evening. Arrangements can be done the day before but must be refrigerated overnight so that they hold nicely.

Pavé bouquets continue to be popular with brides and bridesmaids. Often they too are designed using an abundance of a single type of flower. Our

(Above) Pavé tulips make for a simply stunning bridal bouquet. Ribbon wraps the stems for ease in carrying and to protect the bride's hands.

bride holds a pavé of double white tulips. The designer simply begins with a single blossom (all leaves are removed) around which concentric circles of blooms are added one at a time until the ideal shape and size of the bouquet materializes. When this is done carefully and compactly a beautifully domed cap of flowers evolves naturally.

(Opposite) Our team created these trays of pavé roses to hold place cards at the wedding of a music industry executive. Long wooden boxes were painted white and allowed to dry. Trays were lined with plastic sheeting, filled with wet floral foam, and set into place on the table. (Trays can be suspended or placed at varying heights with risers.) Roses were added and petals strewn—a breathtaking display indeed.

(Above) Nestled inside this blossom are gardenia blooms. The blooms scent the air with their heady fragrance.

BLOOMING IDEA

Cocktail Hour

Today's popular cocktails, especially martinis, are often colorful and visually interesting in their own right but it never hurts to have a little something interesting to put on those sit-down or stand-up cocktail tables. A single blossom floating in a small glass square lined with smooth river rocks could be a sleek alternative design.

Constructed Magnolia Blossom

What you will need

• 4" Styrofoam ball
• 6" bowl
• Damp cloth or leaf-shine product
• Garden snips
• Hot glue gun
• Small magnolia leaves with brown velvet backs, about 12
• Small and medium magnolia leaves, about 12
• White rose or several gardenia blossoms

What you will do

1. Clean leaf surface with damp cloth or use a leaf-shine product (Photo A).
2. Snip stems off leaves (Photo B).
3. Apply hot glue along the back side of a magnolia leaf to the stem (Photo C).
4. Hold the Styrofoam ball in your hand and place the leaf in the mid section of the ball (Photo D). Do the same thing with the second leaf, placing it directly next to the first leaf, overlapping it slightly (Photo E). Continue this process until you have a collar of leaves in the mid section of the ball. The magnolia leaves will be free at the top. (You should be able to look down in and see the top of the Styrofoam ball easily.)
5. Add a second layer of leaves right below the first layer. Be sure they overlap the first row to cover the glued part of those leaves.
6. To finish your blossom, glue small leaves with brown velvet backs for the final row. This time, the leaves will be glued the same way but because they will be placed in a row at the bottom of the ball, they will have a natural tendency to roll out and expose their lovely brown interior.
7. Tuck a few rose petals or gardenia blooms inside the blossom (Photos F and G).
8. Nestle the completed blossom in a bowl and enjoy (Photo H).

A

B

C

D

E

F

G

H

BLOOMING IDEA

Love Me Tender

Never touch gardenia petals without very wet fingers.

Even then you must handle them very gingerly—

they bruise and turn brown easily but their beauty

is well worth the care they demand.

Still-Life Centerpiece

What you will need

- Assorted leaves, vines, and berries
- Bowl for fruit
- Bucket of water
- Candle fitters or floral wax
- Candlesticks with candles, 3
- Containers of varying size and height, 3
- Cut flowers
- Dark bound books without dust jackets
- Floral adhesive tape, clear
- Floral foam blocks, 2
- Fresh fruit: grapes, pears, pomegranates, or figs
- Garden snips
- Hammer
- Moss or paper (if needed)
- Serrated knife

What you will do

1. Using floral adhesive tape, tape grids on tops of containers that will hold tall arrangements (Photos A and B). For shorter arrangements, you will need to add floral foam to the containers (Photo C).
2. Soak floral foam in a bucket of water until it's fully saturated. Then, using a serrated knife, cut floral foam to fit each container. Floral foam should raise about 1" above the rim of container. Add water to containers.

(continued on page 77)

(Opposite) Old World elegance meets modern sophistication in this multi-layered centerpiece.

BLOOMING IDEA

Flowers of the Masters

Choose flowers and other textures in Flemish paintings—tulips, lilies, garden roses, etc. We used red amaryllis, white hydrangea (Photo D), antique blue hydrangea, and red parrot tulips (Photo E), and viburnum.

74

D

E

F

G

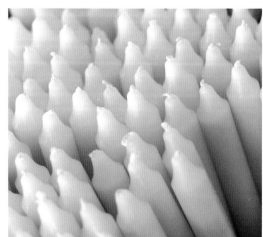

(continued from page 74)

3. Choose one kind of flower for the tallest vase. We chose two stems of red amaryllis for half of our tall vases and four stems of blue hydrangea for the other half. To the red amaryllis we added a couple of stems of fall leaves and to the blue hydrangea we added one stem of viburnum. Hold your stem of flowers up to the vase and decide where you need to snip the stem so that it settles into the vase nicely without being too short. The viburnum stem is a woody stem and needs a bit of pounding so that it takes up water more readily (Photo D). The hydrangea stems get an X-shaped cut (Photo E).

4. Our medium-sized vase was filled with three bunches of red parrot tulips (Photo F). Cut the tulips and put them in one at a time, always aiming each new stem toward the center of the container. (Don't leave tulip stems too long as they will continue to grow, reach for the light, and begin to look too leggy.)

5. Our smallest vase holds antique blue hydrangea cut short with an X cut into the bottom of its stem. The arrangements are now complete (Photo G).

6. Secure the candles in the candlesticks using candle fitters or floral wax.

7. Fill the bowl with fruit, allowing the interesting patches of color and texture on the fruit to show. Create a false bottom of moss or paper if your fruit bowl is deep.

8. Bring together all of the elements of your centerpiece on one table. Cluster the three containers of flowers in the middle of the table. Slide two books under the tallest vase. Put two candlesticks together in one location and place the third candlestick on the other side of the flowers. Add the bowl of fruit to the collection and casually spill some of the fruit onto the table. Light the candles and…voilá!

(Above) The arrangements on the head table honor the bride's love of the color red. Using a single color makes a strong visual impact.

BLOOMING IDEA

Lucky Penny

The place card holder is actually faux fruit. Names were printed on vellum and attached with a shiny decorative nail. To keep the pear from tipping over, a penny was adhered to the bottom using floral wax.

Embellished Tablecloth

What you will need

- Berries, like coffee berries, also known as hypericum (Photo A)
- Carnations
- Floral sticks
- Garden snips
- Glue pan and hot glue
- Patterned 90" round tablecloth
- Red roses (Photo B)
- Round table

What you will do

1. Place tablecloth on table. Decide what part of the pattern you would like to enhance with flowers and repeat that pattern throughout.
2. Snip flower heads and berries from their stems (Photo C).
3. Carefully dip base of flowers or berries into hot glue. Feel free to apply glue to flower base or berries with a floral stick.
4. Hold berry or flower in place for a few seconds to make sure it holds.
5. Repeat Steps 3 and 4 until you are satisfied with the results (Photo D).

(Opposite) No surface was left untouched—even the cake and cake table got dressed up with flowers. The mother of the bride found this fabric while planning the wedding. She loved that it matched the blue and white vases used to hold the arrangements.

Bridal Trellis

What you will need

- Floral wire
- Garden shears
- Magnolia blooms
- Magnolia branches
- Trellis (available at home improvement and garden stores or party rental stores)

What you will do

1. Stake trellis securely in the ground (Photo A).
2. Starting with taller branches, wire branches at seams in trellis and along the sides (Photo B).
3. Fill in empty spots with smaller branches. Secure with wire (Photo C).
4. Pluck magnolia blossoms into spots as desired. Secure with wire if necessary (Photo D).
5. Continue filling in until you are pleased with results. Keep in mind Mother Nature—sometimes simple is best!

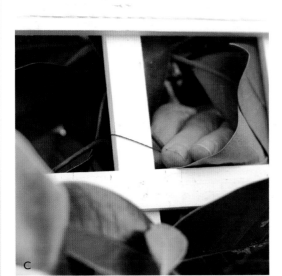

(Opposite) This magnolia trellis is the perfect backdrop to the ceremony. The bride wanted the trellis to blend in with the surroundings.

ADDING STILL-LIFE ELEMENTS

This wedding reception layout features a very long head table to accommodate a large wedding party. In the center of this long expanse was the special round sweetheart table set with wingback chairs for the bride and groom and positioned in front of the mantel.

Because the guests at this table were seated on one side only there was a significant amount of table space crying out for flowers, color, and candlelight. We had bought and prepared the containers and materials for our 22 60" round guest tables and we had planned for eight additional guest tables, which generated enough pieces to decorate the head table.

We did depart from the grouping formula we had used on the guest tables and created a more lyrical grouping of still-life elements more suitable to a long, narrow space. We saved a dynamite grouping of lower red flowers in containers, red bound books, and red fruit for the sweetheart table to set it apart slightly.

Large-scale containers four times the size of our other centerpiece containers were reserved for the mantel, along with whole magnolia branches and long, full bundles of rose hips and red viburnum berries. Massive architectural elements like this mantel literally consume vast quantities of organic materials. Two ladies of the bridal brigade created pieces for the hearth and found the scale rather daunting.

(Top right) Start your arrangements with the containers. Once you are pleased with their placement, add leaves and branches. (Right) For the fireplace, use bigger, more rustic elements than on the tables. The weight of the arrangements helps balance the scale of the fireplace.

(Opposite) The head table holds all the grandeur. Here, we have worked in groupings of three—a set of candles and sets of blue and red arrangements—to give the most visual appeal.

Chapter 5

A Graduation Celebration

The pursuit of education is an admirable and noble one. Since education is a serious subject, I designed a look for a graduation celebration that befits scholarly pursuits. The designs are simple and sophisticated at their core, yet they can be dressed up or down to suit the personality and the gender of the graduate being honored. It is not by accident that the primary accent color shown here is green. Green is the color of new money and new beginnings.

Parents will want to invite family and friends to this party and the graduate will want to invite his or her own friends, so perhaps a buffet lunch is best. Everyone can feel free to eat, mingle, and reminisce in a casual atmosphere.

If your graduate is an athlete it would be fun to have the buffet set up on the football field or tennis court—someplace that honors the student's pursuits. While these may sound ideal, the locations may not be practical. Your home can be just as wonderful.

Most of the projects shown throughout this chapter are organic and sophisticated in nature. They are lightened up with flowers and linens in the school colors. All of the containers are wood, many of them salad bowls. A few accessories add just a touch of whimsy.

(Opposite) Congratulate your graduate with a party designed with school colors in mind. The flower arrangements and embellishments pay tribute to their alma mater.

(Above) For a simple yet pretty arrangement, just plant the succulents and place as needed.

Scotch Moss Checkerboard

What you will need

- 4" dark green Scotch moss plants, 6
- 4" light green Scotch moss plants, 6
- Knife
- Poly foil or plastic sheeting
- Scissors
- Wooden serving tray

What you will do

1. Cut a piece of foil or plastic to line the interior of the serving tray.
2. Remove the moss plants from their pots and carefully slice off half of the soil ball.
3. Position them in the tray close to each other, alternating light and dark plants until the tray is plump with a checkerboard moss cushion.

Arrangement of Succulents

What you will need

- 4" succulents, 8
- Large wooden salad bowl
- Poly foil or plastic sheeting
- Potting soil
- Scissors

What you will do

1. Line the interior of the salad bowl with a piece of foil or plastic.
2. Remove the succulents from their pots and tuck them into the salad bowl using potting soil to fill in as needed.
3. Add succulents until the surface of the bowl is covered. Push all the plants down firmly into the soil.

(Opposite) This "salad" of moss dresses up the table without being fussy or feminine.

Pavé of Flowers

What you will need

- Block of floral foam
- Bowl of water
- Clumps of mood moss, 5
- Garden snips
- Green pot tape
- Poly foil or plastic sheeting
- Red carnations, 12
- Small wooden salad bowls, 2

What you will do

1. Soak the floral foam until it is saturated. Cut foam to fit bowl—foam should rise about 1" above rim of bowl. Using pot tape, secure foam in bowl.

2. For the pavé of carnations, begin with the wooden bowl that has been prepared with floral foam. The idea is to form a smooth dome of carnations over the surface of the bowl.

3. Snip half of your carnations down until they have 3" stems.

4. Beginning in the center of the bowl, tuck the first flower into the foam, pushing it in about 1". This will be your highest flower.

5. Tuck in the second flower right next to it and then the third flower—always working in a circle around the center flower—aiming the new stems toward the center, the heart of the container.

6. As each new, tight circle of flowers is added, push the stems in a little deeper. This is necessary to cause the dome shape. Snip more carnation stems as you need them. Make the stems a bit shorter as you get closer to the edge of the bowl. The final row of flowers will be resting right on the surface of the floral foam. Their stems need to be shortest of all.

(Above) Holding court next to a bowl of pavé roses is the mascot from our graduate's alma mater. Make your graduation celebration more personal by adhering to school colors, or including the school's song on the invitation.

(Opposite) Carnations are inexpensive and can be dyed to match the colors of the day.

Pavé Dome of Ivy

What you will need

- 4" Styrofoam ball
- All-purpose white glue
- Black marker
- Hot glue gun
- Large ivy leaves, 2 handfuls
- Leaf gloss
- Salad bowl
- Soft cloth

What you will do

1. Trim the stems off the ivy leaves. Discard any new-growth ivy leaves (they are smaller, lighter in color, and thinner to the touch).
2. With a damp cloth, wipe the leaves free of dirt and grime.
3. Cut the 4" Styrofoam ball in half to form a dome and fasten it to the salad bowl with hot glue or earthquake wax.
4. Touch a dab of glue to the stem end of the first ivy leaf. Place the leaf on the lower edge of the Styrofoam dome with the tip of the leaf pointing down. Repeat until you have a single row of leaves all the way around the lower edge of the dome.
5. Add a second row of leaves in the same manner, making certain that you overlap the first row of leaves just enough to cover the dabs of glue. (The ivy leaf will turn black right where the hot glue is placed.)
6. Continue until the Styrofoam dome is completely covered with layers of leaves. Finish the very top of the dome with a couple of leaves glued on with white glue so that no burn marks are allowed to show.

BLOOMING IDEA

Pavé Alternatives

Once you have cut your dome of Styrofoam and have attached it to its base,

you can add a pavé of any number of things. The ivy is gorgeous but the

covering could be red carnations as shown in the center of the photo on

page 88. The base for this dome is simply tall and thin instead of short and

round. Red roses are also hearty enough to gather and display in a low setting.

(Opposite) This new take on ivy adds interest to the graduation table.

Chapter 6

A Friendship Celebration

Luncheons are defined as a formal midday repast. Our luncheon is for a small group of longtime girlfriends. Think of it as a tea party with a distinctively English flair in a shabby and chic setting.

An intimate outdoor room or similar well-lit space is perfect for this celebration—such a space requires little additional embellishment. Garden hooks hung with fabric cones stuffed with violet plants stand in a flower bed. Violets and pansies are the featured flowers of the day, accompanied by other purple flowers, ivies, herbs, and berries.

The guest tables are dressed with layers of heirloom linens. Flowers spill over and fill the mid sections of the tables. Salads and small cakes are garnished with flowers, while the chair backs are appointed with fabric cone favors.

This is the perfect occasion to dig out your mother or grandmother's china and silver and all of those lace and cutwork linens you have been collecting for years. For a shabby yet chic look, use them in layers. Dig in your curio cabinet and pull out your collection of pretty things. Vases, glasses, and teacups look great holding flowers, while figurines are good company for the flowers.

Without a doubt, there is plenty for the eyes to feast on. Keep the menu simple and prepare food ahead of time. Also keep in mind that the food should be just as gorgeous as your setting.

(Opposite) A pretty patio is the backdrop for our girlfriends' get-together. The lush greenery provides shade and privacy.

Fabric Cone of Violets

(Above) The deep purple hue of the African violets is a stunning contrast to the green of the cone and moss.

What you will need

- 1"-wide ribbon, 3 yards
- 4" purple African violet plants, 3
- 6" plastic garden pot
- Black marker
- Fabric, 1 yard
- Garden hook
- Hot glue gun
- Moss
- Pencil
- Potting soil
- Scissors
- Spray adhesive
- White poster board

What you will do

1. Cut your poster board to 24" x 36".
2. Lay your fabric down, wrong side up. Spray the surface with adhesive and lay the poster board shape on the tacky surface. Cut around the shape, leaving 1" of extra fabric all the way around. Pick up the shape and carefully fold the extra inch back over the edge of the shape and hot glue in place; set aside to dry.
3. Hold the shape on the bottom in the center. Push the lower left-hand corner up toward the center line of the shape until you can see the lower point of a cone beginning to form. Roll the right-hand side of the shape around the left side, always maintaining the point at the bottom of the cone.
4. Test the size of your cone by placing the 4" pot inside the top of the cone. It should fit in snugly. If it doesn't fit, you need to release the wrap slightly. When everything fits just right, touch the small flap that has come around toward the front of the cone with hot glue to secure the proper shape. Reach down inside the cone with the glue gun and secure the flaps there.
5. Cut the ribbon into two 1-yard lengths. One yard of ribbon is used to hang the cone from the garden hook (be certain to glue the ends securely at the top of the cone). The remainder of the ribbon is divided and used as added embellishment.
6. Plant all three African violet plants in the 4" pot so it looks lush and full. Tuck in moss where any soil can be seen.
7. Carefully lower the pot of violets into the fabric cone.
8. Pull the two loops of ribbon up together, carefully avoiding the violet leaves because they snap easily.
9. Place the garden hook in the ground. Hang the cone by its ribbons and add additional ribbons if you like.

(Opposite) We've taken a new approach to hanging baskets by creating this exquisite floral cone. Planting flowers in a pot allows them to be taken out of the cone for watering, so you can enjoy the cone throughout the spring and summer.

Stacked Teacups with Flowers

What you will need

- Floral adhesive tape
- Floral foam
- Garden snips
- Hot glue pan and glue
- Lavender flowers
- Moss
- Popsicle stick
- Purple pansy plants, 4-6
- Stem of scented geranium
- Teacups and saucers, 2

What you will do

1. Prepare one of the teacups with floral foam. The floral foam should rise above the cup about 2". Tape around the rim of the cup, tape across the top of the cup in both directions, then finish by taping around the rim one more time.

2. Put a glob of hot glue with Popsicle stick where the tape crosses on top of the teacup. Set the saucer of a second teacup set on top of the glue; allow the glue to set.

3. Cut the blossoms off of a few stems of lavender flowers. Tuck them into the floral foam, below the saucer just glued on, until the foam is covered with blossoms. Add touches of scented geranium.

4. Plant the second teacup with pansies. Hide any soil with moss and put the teacup on the empty saucer.

(Opposite and above right) Orphan teacups and saucers can be found at antiques and thrift stores and flea markets. If you don't have time to hunt for a vintage set, purchase new, inexpensive ones at a department or discount store.

(Bottom right) Our celebration includes lots of lush purple flowers including pansies.

THE ROOT OF THE CONE

Have you every stopped to think how many good things come tucked into cone shapes?

Expensive ice cream is scooped into waffle cones, brightly colored shaved ice is plopped atop short, fat paper cones, and cotton candy is spun onto long, thin paper cones. At the turn of the last century, Victorian ladies filled fancy paper and lace cones with fruit and nuts and created pretty little flower nosegays in their delicate cone-shaped tussie mussie holders. It is apparent that the cone must have a long, delightful history.

Cones have a history with me. As children, my friends and I would deliver our handmade treasures and then we would ring the doorbell and run like the wind, or so it seemed. Every May 1st I feel obliged to create a few decorated cones laced with ribbons and filled with fresh flowers and candies to hang on my neighbors' doorknobs. The ringing and running parts, though, no longer seem necessary.

It is of no surprise to me that cones filled with flower petals are considered a nice sentimental touch to include when planning a wedding. Party planner Alyson Fox made certain that Britney Spears had lovely beaded cones that could be kept as mementos of an exceptional evening.

The cones for our luncheon were covered with a moss-colored suede fabric—soft and subtle—so that the textures and colors of the pansies and violets could really shine through. The favors on the chair backs could have also been filled with candies or little trinkets and gifts resting in a bed of excelsior.

(Above) Mix and match china and silver to celebrate the feminine mystique.

(Below) Today flower-filled paper cones are hung from chairs, hooks, along the aisles leading up to the wedding ceremony site—just about anywhere you can imagine.

(Opposite) Fresh blooms on and near the luncheon table add fragrance and beauty only best friends would truly appreciate.

Favor Cone for Chair Back

What you will need

- 1"-wide ribbon for each cone, 1 yard
- Hot glue gun
- Poster board
- Scissors
- Spray adhesive
- Tarp or paper to protect work surface
- Upholstery-weight fabric, 1/2-yard
- Violas or pansy blooms

What you will do

1. For each cone cut a 10" x 12" rectangle from the poster board.
2. Cut a square of fabric a couple of inches larger than the poster board and lay it face down on the protected surface of the table.
3. Spray the fabric with adhesive and lay the poster board shape on top of it. Trim around the edges, leaving a 1" margin of fabric.
4. Fold the 1" margin back over the edge of the poster board so edges of cone are finished; set in place with hot glue.
5. Roll into cone shape and hot glue into place.
6. Hot glue 12" ribbon to the top of the inside of opposite sides of cone. This will serve as the handle or tie (Photo A).
7. Cross ribbon and tie into a bow at the bottom of cone.
8. Embellish with additional ribbon (Photo B).
9. Trim edges of ribbon at an angle (Photo C).
10. Hang cone on chair (Photo D).
11. Fill cone with pansies, violas, or other small purple flowers (Photo E).

(Opposite) Traditionally filled with candy, we planted our favor cones with flowers instead.

Flower Garnishes

What you will need

- Edible, organic flowers (violets and pansies)
- Fruit, star fruit, strawberries, or passion fruit slices
- Little cakes or petite fours
- Paintbrush, small
- Paper towel
- Parchment paper
- Pasteurized egg whites
- Raspberry vinaigrette dressing
- Salad of fresh spring baby greens
- Salt
- Small bowl
- Superfine sugar
- Toasted walnut halves
- Tweezers

What you will do

1. Order organic pansies from a local health food market or specialty market or gather from a garden where you know pesticides have not been used.
2. Pick the most perfect, fully opened flowers early in the morning, before the sun wilts the flowers. Pick some blooms for your salad and some to sugar for your cakes. Use the flowers with the longest stems for your salad. To keep fresh until used in the salad, put flowers in a tiny vase of water and store in a cool location.
3. Prepare your salad as you normally would, but this time garnish it with fruit slices and scatter a few fresh flowers among the greens.

(continued on page 104)

(Opposite) Now is the perfect time to break out your grandmother's tea service. Use it in her memory and in honor of the years of friendship at your friendship celebration. The tradition of sugared flowers hearkens back to the days of our female ancestors and adds a surprising and pretty touch to petite fours (top right) and a delicious salad (bottom right).

(Above) These lovely linens were special-ordered just for the luncheon. However, there are many ways to procure what is needed for a memorable tabletop.

(continued from page 103)

4. Follow Sugaring Blooms instructions to sugar some violets and pansies to decorate the cakes. Do these ahead as they will store nicely for some time.

Sugaring Blooms

1. Bathe the flowers you are going to sugar in cool water. (Add a pinch of salt to the water beforehand.)

2. Remove flowers from water and give them a quick dip in ice-cold water to harden the petals; allow to dry on paper towel.

3. Pour pasteurized egg whites into a small bowl and dilute with a bit of water.

4. Hold each flower with a pair of tweezers. With a clean, small paintbrush, apply a thin, even layer of egg white over the entire surface of the flower, both front and back. Be sure that you don't miss any spots.

5. Sift superfine sugar onto flowers using your fingers or a shaker.

6. Cover each flower thoroughly, then tap the tweezers to cause excess sugar to fall.

7. Move the flowers to a piece of sugar-covered parchment paper. Let dry about 4 hours. The larger pansies will probably need to be shifted around after a couple of hours or flipped over so they dry thoroughly.

8. If you do sugar the flowers ahead of time, store them in an airtight container between layers of waxed paper.

9. Top each petit four with a sugared bloom.

10. Place fresh, edible flowers on salad just before serving.

THE SEARCH IS ON

Not everyone is a collector of pretty things, but you can still pull off the look featured here. Whether you are looking to replace one broken dish, locate the perfect tea set, or want to find linens for your party, there is a place out there that has it.

If you enjoy collecting china pieces, antique linens, and various silver patterns, how about a day spent antiquing or flea-market shopping with your girlfriends? Take advantage of the time together and ask for their input regarding the party planning.

In your search for linens there is a good chance that you will run across white hemstitched linen napkins. In lieu of a placecard, have each guest's name or monogram machine embroidered onto a hemstitched napkin.

Share your love of old silver with your friends. As you peruse antique sources choose an assortment of teaspoons with lovely patterns and place one with each teacup and saucer

at the table. Invite your guests to take the teaspoons with them as a special memento of the day.

If you own a favorite china, silver, or crystal pattern (even if it is discontinued) and you would like to replace a chipped or broken piece, or you would like to add to your collection before your scheduled luncheon, by all means turn to your computer. Internet search engines can steer you in the right direction. There are literally thousands of replacement sources available.

If your guest list grows larger than the number of place settings you had planned for, you can always turn to a company that rents everything you need—from tables, chairs, and linens to china, flatware, and stemware.

(Right) Don't have your grandmother's silver? You can find silver to suit your style in many different ways—from flea-market jaunts and antique store quests to online catalog searches.

Chapter 7

A Cultural Celebration

The world is a melting pot of cultures. Immigrants come to our shores with their own set of special celebrations, traditions, and recipes. They move to our cities and into neighborhoods where others from their homeland live. They establish businesses like restaurants, grocery stores, and import shops that feature the cuisine and products from their corner of the world. If you watch television much, especially cable television, you have witnessed a literal explosion of diverse cooking shows and the rising popularity of gourmet clubs. We now have a plethora of information about the traditions and cuisine of any culture as well as an influx of resources from which to acquire the ingredients and decor to experience those cultures right in our own homes.

This chapter features a dinner party designed with an ethnic lifestyle in mind. Brave hosts and hostesses among us take the time to study cookbooks and to prepare dishes that are not familiar to our palates. Others only take time to "order out" favorite ethnic food. And, as far as I'm concerned, there is nothing wrong with the later approach.

Our dinner party celebrates the culture and cuisine of India. The color palette is a strong one—hot pink, saffron yellow, orange, and metallic gold. Marigolds are the flowers of choice simply because they are synonymous with the culture and they possess dynamite color. Colorful sheer fabrics and lots of candlelight lend an exotic, mystical air.

(Opposite) To create our dining pavilion, we built a temporary structure of four wood pillars joined at the top and sides by 2" x 8' boards. We covered the wood pillars with brightly colored silk and draped sheer fabric over the boards.

SHORT AND STUNNING

This project is undoubtedly the most simple of projects yet it is as beautiful and as striking as any of the other more complicated flower designs in this book.

The trick is to find a beautiful bowl short in stature and the single most beautiful flower that you have ever seen.

The arrangement can most certainly be repeated several times on the same table and because of the nature of the design the cost can be modest, unless of course you choose an art glass piece as your bowl, which by the way would be spectacular.

(Above) The bright colors of the fabrics call for simple arrangements on the table. What can be easier than floating a few candles and flowers in a shallow bowl?

Floating Flowers and Candles

What you will need
- Large, exquisite flower
- Large shallow bowl, metal or glass
- Several floating candles

What you will do

1. Put this arrangement together after your dinner table is set at the party location. Sloshing water is not good for the candle wicks or the gorgeous bloom.
2. Fill the bowl 2/3 with water, then add the candles and the flower. The arrangement is complete!

(Above) Huge pink peonies or fragrant orange garden roses are perfect choices for this simple arrangement.

(Opposite) Part of the charm of this simple arrangement is the fact that we are mesmerized by the sparkling water in which the flowers and candles are floating. This also is the perfect opportunity to showcase one very special bloom—an open peony, a plate-sized dahlia, or the most gorgeous open garden rose you have ever seen.

Flower Chains

What you will need

- Assorted brass beads and hot glue gun (optional)
- Dental floss, 45" length
- Garden snips
- Long needle with a medium eye
- Marigold blossoms, 50, or carnations, 30

What you will do

1. Snip all of the flower heads off of their stems, right where their calyx joins the stem.
2. Thread the dental floss through the eye of your needle. A single strand is sufficient.
3. Thread the needle down through the middle of the first blossom and out through the green calyx. Slide the blossom down until it reaches the bottom of the dental floss. Leave a 4" strand of floss at the end. Take an extra stitch crossways of the calyx to secure the first blossom on the chain (the next flower will cover that stitch).
4. Continue threading the other blooms in the same manner—through the head and out through the calyx—until you have a chain of flowers about 36" long. If you would like, finish off the end with a series of beads. A bit of hot glue inside the beads will secure them on the floss or you can pull the end around and make a lei instead of a chain.

BLOOMING IDEA

Quick Thinking

I was a bit late in the season to find marigolds

easily so on this single occasion I decided

that it would be OK to mix silk and fresh

flowers. I still had the luxury of the marigold's

pungent fragrance but I also had the volume

of flowers necessary for the project.

(Opposite) Reminiscent of the daisy chains made in childhood, our grown-up version is a time-honored tradition in India. Flower leis can be joined end-to-end (top right), and laid along the table (middle and bottom right).

Fabric-Covered Glass Cylinders

What you will need

- Carnations, optional
- Fabric scissors
- Glass cylinders, assorted sizes
- Hot glue gun
- Pencil
- Pillar candles, 3" x 3" or 3" x 6"
- Scissors
- Scrap paper to make a pattern
- Sheer fabric (1 yard covers nine 10" cylinders)

What you will do

1. Make a pattern for each cylinder size by measuring the height of your first cylinder. Use that figure to measure off width of paper (if your cylinder is 10" tall, measure 11" and cut on the line).
2. Roll this length of paper around your cylinder. Notice where the paper meets and make a small mark.
3. Remove the paper from the cylinder and lay it on the table.
4. Draw a straight line down from the mark you made, add an extra inch and then cut on that line. This is the pattern you will use to cut the fabric to cover the cylinder.
5. Repeat this process for each cylinder.
6. Lay the pattern down on your fabric and snip the salvage edge at the edge of the pattern. Tear this piece of fabric across until it comes free. Again, lay your pattern on this strip of fabric and cut the lengths you will need.
7. Repeat this process for each cylinder.
8. When all of your fabric is cut you are ready to apply the fabric to the glass. Simply run a straight line of hot glue down the face of the glass cylinder. Lay one edge of your fabric on that line. Allow it to set for a minute and then pull the remainder of the fabric around the cylinder and add a second line of glue right on top of the first line you made.
9. Pull the fabric taut and put down onto the glue. Trim off any excess fabric. Your fabric-covered cylinder is now ready for any additional embelishments you may want to add.
10. For added pizzazz, hot glue flower heads around top of pillar.
11. Insert a 3" x 3" or 3" x 6" pillar candle, depending on the size of your cylinder.

(Opposite and top right) No need for electricity when pretty votives in all sizes light up the room. Here, fabric-covered glass cylinders cast a warm, inviting glow on our cultural celebration. (Above, from left) Mix and match your color choices; finish the rim of your vase with pretty carnations; small blooms are a pretty accent to this tone-on-tone candleholder.

BLOOMING IDEA
A Course in Culture

Visit Indian restaurants in your area to see what exciting dishes they serve and how they decorate their spaces. Go to the library or the bookstore and check out the cookbook section for information on Indian cuisine. Often, cookbooks are picture books that offer ideas on menu items and décor. Visit the travel section of your local library or bookstore and look through picture books about India. Get inspired first and you will not only stimulate your own mind but also the minds and palates of your guests. You could just as easily choose an Italian menu, Chinese menu, Thai menu, or any other ethnic menu for that matter.

(Top and above) Ethnic accessories can be easily found in gift stores, import stores, and on the Internet.

(Opposite) Marianne Weiman-Nelson used the same flowing fabrics and strong color with more formal results for the first night's grand gala that celebrated the official opening of the Disney Concert Hall in Los Angeles.

Chapter 8

A New Life Celebration

The prospect of a new life is most endearing and calls for a special kind of celebration. Attending a baby shower is an emotional experience for most women and it encourages much reflection on the part of the guests. The young women in attendance fantasize about having their own children and what colors they will use in their nursery or what names they will call their babies. Older women reminisce about their children as babies—whether they slept through the night or what they did or didn't have as far as conveniences go.

As children, my sisters and I thought babies came from the cabbage patch. With this in mind, I've put together a shower beginning in the produce department of the supermarket. What goes with cabbage besides kings and corned beef? There are carrots, lettuce, and gardens and Peter Cottontail and Farmer Brown. How about a baby shower with a storybook theme—storybooks about rabbits in particular?

The centerpieces on the guest tables are white garden baskets filled with ornamental kale, lettuce, and cabbage roses in shades of pink and fuchsia. A little rabbit waits at each place setting and a plump cabbage rose rests on the napkin.

The gift table also receives special attention. Rabbits with flower collars hide behind the bicycle basket filled with flowers. A country wagon stands ready to receive gifts for the little one. Have no doubt; the story of this day will have a happy ending.

(Opposite) Since we didn't have a cabbage patch, our storybook-themed baby shower takes place on a garden patio.

Garden Arch

What you will need

- 5-gallon bucket, 2
- 6" ornamental kale, 10
- 6" trailing ivies, 6
- 10' pieces of curly willow, 6
- 25-pound bag of plaster of Paris
- Burlap, 3 yards
- Floral wire
- Hot glue gun
- Packages of polyester batting, 2
- Packaging tape
- Polyester batting
- Scissors
- Stepladder
- Twine

What you will do

1. Using one 5-gallon bucket, mix the plaster of Paris following the directions (be certain to add the plaster to the water, not vice versa). The bucket should be only half full of water and plaster.

2. Stand three curly willow branches in one bucket of plaster and allow the plaster to set, holding the branches permanently in place. Repeat the process with the second bucket and the second set of branches.

3. Wrap each of the buckets with a roll of polyester batting and hot glue it in place.

4. Cut two 24" squares of burlap, set the buckets on them, and pull the burlap up around the batting-covered bucket. Tuck the burlap over the edge and glue the edges down with hot glue.

(Above) Planted kale introduces the cabbage patch theme.

5. Move the two buckets of branches into place and space them about 4' apart.

6. Standing on a safe stepladder, pull the curly willow branches together at the top, forming a graceful arch, and secure with little bits of floral wire. Wind the odds and ends of curly willow sticking out in and around each other until you like the total effect.

7. Tuck 4" ivies in the buckets and allow the trailers to spill over the burlap.

8. To complete the look, wrap each of the ornamental kale pots in burlap and cluster them around the base of the arch.

(Opposite) Frame a door or the entrance to your garden or patio with a curly willow arch, transporting your guests to a long-ago time of innocence and promise.

GRAND ENTRANCES

The curly willow entrance to the setting for our baby shower represents the thicket that Peter Rabbit must scamper through to reach Farmer Brown's gardens. If it is a bit stark for your taste you can soften the look with the addition of flowers.

This photograph is from a wedding of a noted music mogul at a four-star Los Angeles hotel. The arch was designed as the bride's entrance to her aisle. The gates incorporated into the arch are tied with ribbon and they have been thrown open for the bride.

You are now looking through the arch to the spot where the bride will first appear to begin her walk down the aisle on her way to the ceremonial bower.

This arch began just as our thicket did with a bundle of long curly willow. Magnolia branches were woven into the willow and plastic cages filled with wet floral foam were strapped into place to accept all of the flower stems.

Notice that the flowers are added in clusters in a manner that imitates Mother Nature. It is wise to study the growing patterns of flowers. It takes a special skill to design floral settings that look as though the flowers were planted there previously and allowed to thrive and flourish so that they would be in full bloom on the bride's special day.

BLOOMING IDEA
Willow I Find It?

Curly willow in a large size will probably have to be ordered through your florist. If curly willow is not available, find alternative green branches that will easily bend. In springtime there are long pussy willow and flowering branches that would make a lovely garden arch. Magnolia branches can be found easily; if you don't have a magnolia tree of your own, ask a friendly neighbor if you can trim theirs.

(Opposite) Magnolia branches add weight while white roses, hydrangea, and ribbon make a gracious statement.

(Above right) Branches blooming with seed pods help punctuate the radiant arch.

Planted Wheelbarrow

What you will need

- 6" pots of kale, variegated ivy, and Irish moss
- Mood moss or sheet moss
- Outdoor enamel spray paint (optional)
- Potting soil
- Wheel barrow or full-size wagon

What you will do

1. If you desire, spray paint wheelbarrow or wagon; let dry completely.
2. Pour a layer of potting soil at the bottom of the wheelbarrow or wagon.
3. Remove kale and ivy from pots and "plant" in wheelbarrow or wagon.
4. Tuck moss into any spots where soil shows.

(Top right and left) Both white and purple kale is readily available at fresh produce markets.

(Opposite) The planted wheelbarrow is an unexpected but perfectly placed accompaniment to the day.

Cabbage Patch Centerpiece

What you will need

- 4" wooden picks with wire, 6
- 12"-14" white basket, wicker or wire
- Basket liner or heavy plastic sheeting
- Blocks of floral foam, 2
- Bucket of water
- Dark and light pink roses with large heads, 12
- Floral wire
- Garden snips
- Heads of cabbage or fluffy green lettuce, 2
- Hot glue gun
- Ivy trailers, 8
- Kale plants, 2
- Mood, sheet, or Spanish moss
- Scented geranium stems, 3-4

What you will do

1. Soak floral foam in water and place in basket. If you are using a wire basket, line it with moss first.

2. Tuck the cut end of four ivy trailers in the wet foam at each handle location. Bring them up, one at a time, and twist them around the handle, if your basket has one, crossing them over each other as you go. Secure them at the top with a short piece of floral wire.

3. Snip the big rosettes of ornamental kale off of their root system, leaving as long a stem as possible. If the plant is very mature, the stem will be long enough to put directly into the wet foam. If not, you will need to push a 4" wooden pick into the stem that does exist to extend its length. If the rosette is really heavy, add a second pick at an angle going right directly into the head of the kale from below.

4. Place the kale in your basket.

5. Push wooden picks into the stem end of the cabbage or lettuce. Add these to your basket, positioning them close to the kale for a clustered effect.

6. Tuck a few shorter trailers of ivy into the basket.

7. Add the roses one at a time, giving each one a fresh new cut. Space them out across the surface of the basket as you go. If there is still floral foam showing, tuck in a few clippings of scented geranium.

8. Hot glue bits of moss to the handle, if your basket has one, where any wires can be seen.

(Above) Wooden picks inserted into cabbage hold the vegetables securely in place. Fill in any empty spaces with full leaves.

(Opposite) Garden vegetables are woven into the centerpiece arrangement, while Peter Cottontail awaits the guests' arrival!

HERE COMES PETER COTTONTAIL

The beloved nursery character, Peter Cottontail, inspired our tabletop theme. Each of the elements pay tribute to this cheeky rabbit—moss serves as grass, flowers that line his path are the focal point, and Peter himself makes an appearance in the form of a ceramic bunny at each place setting.

This beautifully laden tableau is perfect for an indoor sunroom, a backyard garden, or even under a grand oak. Many of the items can be found in your yard or kitchen. Fresh vegetables are fodder for the creative mind, providing the very scene Peter Cottontail may encounter on his bunny trail.

Springtime is a wonderful time to celebrate with a Peter Cottontail theme. This is a time of rebirth, a season where fields are profuse with fresh flowers and grasses are recovering from the dormancy of winter. This is the moment to embrace life and its new offerings.

BLOOMING IDEA

Nursery Rhyme Inspiration

If you're at a loss for nursery rhyme-inspired ideas, head to your local library or bookstore for a refresher course in some of the most beloved children's stories.

Once a theme or rhyme is chosen, consider creating bookmarks with the rhyme printed on them. Simply print the title and words from a computer on cardstock, cut it out, hole punch the top, and add a ribbon. For an easy-to-make centerpiece, stack a number of children's books, finishing with a floral arrangement or potted plant on top.

(Above) Our little bunny figurines were purchased at a crafts store. You could also use a childhood collection of storybook animals to decorate the table.

(Opposite, clockwise from top) A low iron container allows moss to peak out; while moss is available in different colors, only the greenest green will do; roses take any centerpiece up a notch.

Working With Specialty Roses

There are roses on the market that resemble English garden roses. They have many, many circles of petals on their interior. Latin Ambience is one of my favorites. This rose is perfect for the project. Purchase your roses the day before you need them. Trim the stems and put them in warm water. Your roses will be more open and showy when you are ready to add them to the basket. If you have roses that are already open, keep them in cold water until you are ready to place them in arrangements.

(Below) A table blooming with fresh flowers is a beautiful table indeed.

Cabbage Rose on Napkin

What you will need

- Garden snips
- Large-head open rose
- Napkin

What you will do

1. Begin with the outermost petals of the rose. One at a time, with your thumb and first finger, encourage the petals to roll outward. This is called reflexing, and it takes a gentle touch.
2. Continue turning the petals out until you have a nice plump look to your rose.
3. Snip off the stem and place the rose on the napkin.

(Opposite) The key to this project is to have a rose that is open enough to be able to work with its inner petals. Pictured here is a fragrant Yves Piaget rose.

A

B

C

Floral Collars for Rabbits

What you will need

- 4" pot of ivy with long trailers
- Garden snips
- Green chenille or pipe cleaner, 1-2 per rabbit
- Hot glue gun
- Small blossoms, roses, carnations, or daisies

What you will do

1. Make a ring out of the chenille to fit the rabbit's neck loosely.

2. Snip some of the shorter trailers from the ivy plant (Photo A). Twine them around the chenille one at a time; they will probably cling to the chenille without needing to fasten them. Add ivy until you have a nice shape.

3. Snip the tiny flowers off of their stems (Photos B and C).

4. Hot glue flowers onto the wreath (Photo D). The flowers will stick better on the chenille than on the leaves (Photo E).

D

E

(Opposite) Dress up a plain ceramic bunny with a pretty floral collar. All you need are small blooms, ivy, and chenille or pipe cleaners.

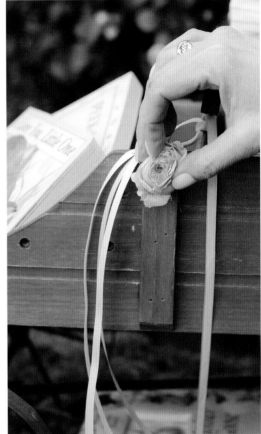

Country Wagon

What you will need

• Books

• Garden snips

• Hot glue pan and glue pellets

• Miniature or child-size wagon

• Pink roses, small

• Thin, double-sided satin ribbon, 4 yards

What you will do

1. Snip the flowers off of their stems and hot glue them onto the wagon.

2. Tie ribbon to the handles and at the top of the seat.

3. Place a few books on the seat of the wagon and underneath. Select book titles that reflect the theme of the day.

(Opposite) An old wagon makes a wonderful receiving table for colorfully wrapped gifts.

(Above, clockwise from top) Attach blooms to stand-out elements of wagon; add each bloom one at a time, starting at the top; satin ribbon beautifully accents the floral embellishments.

(Above) The arrangement for the bicycle features green leafy lettuce and kale paired with roses. The lettuce at top was tucked in at the last minute—there's no need to wire or stake it in.

(Below) Extra heads of cabbbage fill the table space.

(Opposite) The tabletop was covered with plastic sheeting then a layer of heavy-duty craft paper, its edges secured underneath with tape.

BLOOMING IDEA

Covering it Perfectly

Creating your own garden-top table is easy. Begin with a table or console that you already have but make a trip to your local hardware store, where they can cut a matching secondary top out of particle board. This will be the top that you cover with moss. Soak mood moss in water, press out the excess water, and hot glue the mood moss onto the surface. Place your table in its location at the party, protect its top with waterproof padding, and then carefully place your mossed top on it.

About the Author

For more than 20 years, Cindy Smith has plunked, snipped, and dipped her way to the top of her art. Her achievements and her reputation have attracted clients and fans from both the corporate and entertainment worlds. She has designed for Clint Black, Cher, Eddie Murphy, Bruce Springsteen, Sting, and Elizabeth Taylor, as well as celebrity brides Geena Davis, Nicole Kidman, Brooke Shields, Britney Spears, and Tori Spelling. As part of the team of designers at Mark's Garden, Cindy has designed flowers for the most elaborate wedding in prime-time television—the wedding of ABC's Bachelorette Trista and Ryan Sutter, as well as florals for the Academy Awards Governor's Ball.

Cindy is educated in the arts and has taught students from elementary and high school levels and was invited to teach classes at the Smithsonian and the Mennenger Foundation.

When she isn't in her studio in Los Angeles, she is working at her home in the Pacific Northwest. It is here, overlooking the Columbia River, that Cindy is refreshed and re-inspired by the lush vegetation and floral life that surrounds her.

Red Lips 4 Courage
Communications, Inc.:

Eileen Cannon Paulin, Catherine Risling,
Rebecca Ittner, Jayne Cosh

8502 E. Chapman Ave., 303
Orange, CA 92869
www.redlips4courage.com

Book Editor:
Rebecca Ittner

Copy Editor:
Catherine Risling

Book Designer:
Deborah Kehoe
Kehoe + Kehoe Design Associates, Inc.
Burlington, VT

Photographers:
Denny Nelson
Brian Kramer
Simone & Martin
John Solano

Acknowledgments

Thank you to Kitty and Ken for opening the door. Thanks to Mark and Richard for allowing the door to stay open. Love to Drew and Brian for pushing me through that open door. Love to my editor, Rebecca, and my photographer, Denny, for being on the other side.

I'm just one member of an inspired team of fine designers working in a flower studio called Mark's Garden. The images seen throughout this book reflect a conglomeration of everyone's ideas. Thank you design team! Mark Held, Jonnie Ryan, Nancy Kaye, Ingrid Zachs Saxon, Shari Nahid, Joseph Arias, Glenn Hughes, Marco Calderon, Kevin Inkawhich, and Chris Thompson.

To the notable event planners who provide the divine opportunities to design for the wealthy and famous: Mark Held, of Mark's Garden; Mindy Weiss, of Mindy Weiss Party Consultants; Alyson Fox and Diane Levine, of Levine-Fox Events; and Mariane Weiman-Nelson, of Special Occasions, Inc.

A special thank you to Doug and Carol Mancino and Sandra Crosby for allowing us to come into your homes and lives with a camera.

And thanks to those who worked by my side to get flowers in place: Vicky Claybaugh, Shanaz, Chris DeSimone, Nancy, Rebecca, Edwin, and Oleg.

Photography Credits

Denny Nelson Photography
Pasadena, CA
www.dennynelson.com
www.blossomtrailphotography.com

Contributing Photographers

Brian Kramer Photography & Digital Events
Sherman Oaks, CA
www.briankramer.net
Pages 70, 120

John Solano Photography
Los Angeles, CA
www.imagemakr.com
Pages 29, 36, 37

Simone & Martin Photography
Los Angeles, CA
www.simonemartin.com
Page 45

Resources

EVENT PLANNERS
Mark's Garden
Mark Held and Nancy Kaye
Sherman Oaks, CA
www.marksgarden.net
www.marksflowers.com

Mindy Wiess Party Consultants
Beverly Hills, CA
www.mindywiess.com

Levine Fox Events
Alyson Fox and Diane Levine
www.levinefoxevents.com

Marianne Weiman-Nelson
Special Occasions, Inc.
Beverly Hills, CA
www.soievents.com

FABRIC AND RIBBON
Michael Levine
Los Angeles, CA

Top Ten Textile
Los Angeles, CA

FLORAL SUPPLIES
G.M. Floral Co.
Los Angeles, CA

FRESH FLOWERS
Mayesh Wholesale Florist, Inc.
Los Angeles, San Diego, CA, and
Las Vegas

**GLASS AND CERAMIC
CONTAINERS**
Jaygee Sales
San Fernando, CA

LINENS
Ruth Fischl Linens
New York City, NY
www.ruthfischl.com

Resource One, Inc.
Reseda, CA and New York, NY
www.resourceone.info

PARTY RENTALS
Classic Party Rentals
www.regalrents.com

PLANTS
Kobata Growers, Inc.
Torrance, CA
www.kobatagrowers.com

TABLETOP
Unique Tabletop Rentals
www.uniquetabletoprentals.com

Metric Equivalency Chart

inches to millimeters and centimeters
mm-millimeters cm-centimeters

inches	mm	cm	inches	cm	inches	cm
⅛	3	0.3	9	22.9	30	76.2
¼	6	0.6	10	25.4	31	78.7
½	13	1.3	12	30.5	33	83.8
⅝	16	1.6	13	33.0	34	86.4
¾	19	1.9	14	35.6	35	88.9
⅞	22	2.2	15	38.1	36	91.4
1	25	2.5	16	40.6	37	94.0
1¼	32	3.2	17	43.2	38	96.5
1½	38	3.8	18	45.7	39	99.1
1¾	44	4.4	19	48.3	40	101.6
2	51	5.1	20	50.8	41	104.1
2½	64	6.4	21	53.3	42	106.7
3	76	7.6	22	55.9	43	109.2
3½	89	8.9	23	58.4	44	111.8
4	102	10.2	24	61.0	45	114.3
4½	114	11.4	25	63.5	46	116.8
5	127	12.7	26	66.0	47	119.4
6	152	15.2	27	68.6	48	121.9
7	178	17.8	28	71.1	49	124.5
8	203	20.3	29	73.7	50	127.0

yards to meters

yards	meters	yards	meters	yards	meters	yards	meters	yards	meters
⅛	0.11	2⅛	1.94	4⅛	3.77	6⅛	5.60	8⅛	7.43
¼	0.23	2¼	2.06	4¼	3.89	6¼	5.72	8¼	7.54
⅜	0.34	2⅜	2.17	4⅜	4.00	6⅜	5.83	8⅜	7.66
½	0.46	2½	2.29	4½	4.11	6½	5.94	8½	7.77
⅝	0.57	2⅝	2.40	4⅝	4.23	6⅝	6.06	8⅝	7.89
¾	0.69	2¾	2.51	4¾	4.34	6¾	6.17	8¾	8.00
⅞	0.80	2⅞	2.63	4⅞	4.46	6⅞	6.29	8⅞	8.12
1	0.91	3	2.74	5	4.57	7	6.40	9	8.23
1⅛	1.03	3⅛	2.86	5⅛	4.69	7⅛	6.52	9⅛	8.34
1¼	1.14	3¼	2.97	5¼	4.80	7¼	6.63	9¼	8.46
1⅜	1.26	3⅜	3.09	5⅜	4.91	7⅜	6.74	9⅜	8.57
1½	1.37	3½	3.20	5½	5.03	7½	6.86	9½	8.69
1⅝	1.49	3⅝	3.31	5⅝	5.14	7⅝	6.97	9⅝	8.80
1¾	1.60	3¾	3.43	5¾	5.26	7¾	7.09	9¾	8.92
1⅞	1.71	3⅞	3.54	5⅞	5.37	7⅞	7.20	9⅞	9.03
2	1.83	4	3.66	6	5.49	8	7.32	10	9.14

Index

A

Anniversary Celebration 30-47

Arrangement in Iron Urn 38-39

Arrangement of Succulents 87

B

Baskets 48, 54-55

Berries 50-51, 62-65, 78-79

Birthday Celebration 14-29

Bridal Bouquet 71

Bridal Brigade 60-61

Bridal Trellis 80-81

Britney Spears 29, 36, 44

C

Cabbage Patch Centerpiece 124-127

Cabbage Rose on Napkin 128-129

Cake Stand How To 26-27

Candles 56-57, 58, 75-77, 82-83, 107-109, 112-113

Carnations 22-24, 26, 84-85, 88-89, 106, 110-113

Centerpieces 15, 22, 30, 56-57, 58, 74-77, 82-83, 88, 90, 116, 124-125

Cindy Smith 5, 137

Cones 36, 92, 94-95, 98-101

Constructed Magnolia Blossom 72-73

Country Wagon 132-133

Cultural Celebration 106-115

Curly Willow 50-51, 118-121

E

Embellished Garden Hook 18-19

Embellished Pillow 68-69

Embellished Tablecloth 78-79

Extending Flower Life 34

F

Fabric-Covered Boxes 26-27, 40

Fabric-Covered Glass Cylinders 112-113

Fabric Cone of Violets 94-95

Favor Cone for Chair Back 98-101

Fireplace Mantel 54-55

Floating Flowers and Candles 108-109

Floral Birthday Cake Stand 26-27

Flower Chains 110-111

Flower Collars for Rabbit 130-131

Flower Garnishes 102-104

Friendship Celebration 92-105

Fruit Arrangements 50-53, 65

Fruit and Flower Door Basket 32-33

G

Garden Arch 118-121

Gardenias 72-73

Gerbera Daisies 20-23

Glass Vases Filled with Roses 34-35

Graduation Celebration 84-91

Grapes 32-33, 46-47

H

Hanging Flower Basket 18-19

Hanging Votives with Colored Water 42-43

Hot Glue Pan 12

Hydrangeas 18, 38-39, 44-45, 61, 74-76, 82-83, 93, 98

I

Ivy 14, 18-19, 22-23, 90-91, 130-131

K

Kale *118-119, 122-123*

Kate Beckinsale *45*

L

Lemon Topiary *62-65*

Lettuce *124-127*

M

Magnolia Blooms *80-81, 120*

Magnolia Leaves *52, 72-73, 80-81, 120*

Make-Your-Own Centerpiece Station *22-24*

Mantels *44, 48, 58, 83*

Marigolds *110-111*

Moss *10, 18-19, 32-33, 38-39, 66-67, 86-87, 94-95, 122-127, 134-135*

Moss-Covered Table *134-135*

N

New Life Celebration *116-136*

O

Oranges with Cloves *57*

P

Pansies *92, 96-104*

Pavé Dome of Ivy *90-91*

Pavé of Flowers *88-89*

Pavé Roses *70*

Peonies *108-109*

Pillows Talk *68-69*

Planted Wheelbarrow *122-123*

Presents Table *134-135*

R

Reflexing Blooms *40-41, 129*

Reunion Celebration *48-57*

Ribbon Windsock *16-17*

Risers *37, 40*

Rose Topiary Balls *114*

Roses *14, 26-27, 32-40, 44-47, 68-71, 79, 124-135*

S

Scotch Moss Checkerboard *86-87*

Sitting Pretty Bench *66-67*

Slip Knot How To *16*

Stacked Teacups with Flowers *96-97*

Still Life Centerpiece *74-77*

Sugaring Blooms *104*

Sunflowers *48, 54*

T

Tangerine Topiary Tree *50-54*

Tools *10-11*

Tulips *61, 71, 74-77*

V

Violets *92, 94-95*

Votives *42-45*

W

Wedding Celebration *58-83*

Wine Case Favors *46-47*

Wood Picks in Fruit How To *50-53, 65*